Cooking Light

CHICKEN
COOKBOOK

COMPILED AND EDITED BY
SUSAN M. McINTOSH, M.S., R.D.

Oxmoor House

Library of Congress Control Number: 00-136675
ISBN: 0-8487-2493-3
Printed in the United States of America
Third Printing 2002

Previously published as *Low-Fat Ways to Cook Chicken*
  © 1995 by Oxmoor House, Inc.

Editor-in-Chief: Nancy J. Fitzpatrick
Editorial Director, Special Interest Publications: Ann H. Harvey
Senior Foods Editor: Katherine M. Eakin
Senior Editor, Editorial Services: Olivia Kindig Wells
Art Director: James Boone

COOKING LIGHT® CHICKEN COOKBOOK

Menu and Recipe Consultant: Susan McEwen McIntosh, M.S., R.D.
Copy Editor: Catherine Hamrick
Editorial Assistants: Kelly Hooper Troiano, Julie A. Cole
Assistant Foods Editor: Kathryn Matuszak, R.D.
Indexer: Mary Ann Laurens
Assistant Art Director: Cynthia R. Cooper
Designer: Carol Damsky
Senior Photographer: Jim Bathie
Photographers: Howard L. Puckett, Ralph Anderson
Senior Photo Stylist: Kay E. Clarke
Photo Stylists: Cindy Manning Barr, Virginia R. Cravens
Production and Distribution: Phillip Lee
Production Manager: Gail Morris
Associate Production and Distribution Manager: John Charles Gardner
Associate Production Manager: Theresa L. Beste
Production Assistant: Marianne Jordan

Cover: *Chicken Breasts with Mushroom Sauce (Recipe follows on page 114)*
Frontispiece: *Glazed Roasted Chicken (Recipe follows on page 80)*

To order additional publications, call 1-800-633-4910.
For more books to enrich your life, visit
oxmoorhouse.com

Cooking Light®
CHICKEN
COOKBOOK

CONTENTS

CHICKEN PRIMER

*W*hat better way to get started with a low-fat eating plan than to discover more than 150 recipes for ever popular, nutritious chicken! Chicken is a high-protein, vitamin-rich food that is low in total fat, saturated fat, and cholesterol. It is economical, easy to prepare, and extremely versatile—as well suited for a quick lunchbox sandwich as for a special dinner.

AT THE SUPERMARKET

Knowing about the sizes and cuts of chicken available will help you select the leanest and most appropriate choice.

• For most recipes, you can substitute one cut for another—just remember that chicken pieces with the bone require longer cooking times than boned pieces. (Remove skin before cooking to reduce the fat.)

Although a whole broiler-fryer usually costs less per pound, you may prefer to buy specific chicken parts to suit your preference for white or dark meat.

• The white meat of chicken has less fat than the dark. But even the dark meat of chicken is lower in fat than many cuts of red meat and certainly has a place in low-fat meals. For example, Crispy Drumsticks in the Kids in Charge menu (page 14) provide only 27 percent of the calories as fat.

• Small chickens such as broiler-fryers are leaner than roasters, and roasters are leaner than larger hens and capons.

• The less processed a cut of chicken is, the less expensive it will usually be per pound. For instance, you will need 2 cups of chopped cooked chicken for Chicken-Dressing Casserole (page 101). The most economical option is to purchase and cook a whole chicken. However, if short on time, you can spend just a bit more and buy skinned, boned breast halves which can be cooked and chopped more quickly. (See page 10 for basic cooking instructions.)

• Remember that chicken with yellow skin is no more or less nutritious than chicken with pale skin. The skin color is due to the type of feed the chicken is given.

CHOOSING CHICKEN

You will find a wide variety of chicken products available at the meat counter of your supermarket. Choose a whole broiler-fryer for roasting or stewing or specific chicken pieces for a particular recipe. Depending on personal taste, you may prefer a package of dark or white meat only or one of the combination packages to suit the whole family.

• The most economical form of chicken is usually the *Broiler-Fryer*, ranging in weight from 3 to 4½ pounds. As you will see in the recipes to follow, a 3-pound broiler-fryer will usually yield six servings or about 3 cups of chopped, cooked chicken.

• *Young Roasters* are a little larger than broiler-fryers, weighing from 4 to 6 pounds, and are good for oven-roasting and preparing cooked chicken for salads, soups, sandwiches, and casseroles.

• A *Cut-Up Chicken* is a broiler-fryer conveniently cut into pieces: two breast halves, two thighs, two drumsticks, and two wings. Some producers offer a popular combination package of three breast halves, three thighs, and three drumsticks.

• A package of *Chicken Halves* or *Splits* contains two halves of a broiler-fryer. These are ideal for outdoor grilling.

• *Chicken Breast Quarters* and *Leg Quarters* are often packaged separately. A breast quarter is all white meat and includes the wing, breast, and back portion. The leg quarter is all dark meat and includes a drumstick, thigh, and back portion. Each chicken quarter usually yields one serving.

• The *Chicken Breast Half* or *Split Breast* is the leanest cut of chicken. Purchase four (8-ounce) chicken breast halves with bone and skin or four (4-ounce) skinned, boned chicken breast halves for four servings. Two chicken breast halves will yield about 1 cup chopped, cooked chicken.

• The *Chicken Leg* is all dark meat and includes the whole leg with unseparated drumstick and thigh. One chicken leg is considered a serving.

• The *Drumstick* is the lower portion of the chicken leg. Plan to serve 2 drumsticks for each serving.

• The *Thigh* is that portion of the leg above the knee joint. It is usually packaged with skin and bone intact. Skinned, boned thighs may also be available and can usually be substituted for skinned boned chicken breast halves. (You will probably need to cook the thighs longer than the boned breast halves.) Purchase one or two thighs for each serving.

• The *Wing* contains three sections and is all white meat. A *Drummette* is the first section of the wing and is often used for hors d'oeuvres.

• *Ground Chicken*, made from skinned, boned chicken thighs, is available in many supermarkets and is a great alternative to ground beef or ground turkey in meat loaf, soups, or stews. You may also ask your butcher to grind skinned, boned chicken breasts for ground chicken with even less fat. One pound of ground chicken yields four servings.

• In addition, producers often offer other convenient forms such as breast tenderloins, strips, and nuggets, chicken patties, and other semi-prepared and frozen chicken products. Canned chicken is another option for busy cooks. Remember that canned chicken and many of the semi-prepared and frozen products may be high in sodium from added salt or other ingredients.

Skinned, boned poultry may be purchased for convenience. Ground poultry is a lower fat alternative to ground beef.

FOOD SAFETY

Chicken, like any meat, must be handled properly in order to destroy salmonella bacteria that may be present in the uncooked meat. Salmonella that is ingested with food can cause a serious illness that results in flu-like symptoms. It's easy to avoid this problem by cooking the chicken properly and following some basic food-handling practices.

• At the supermarket check the "sell by" date, and choose the freshest product available. The chicken should look and smell fresh.

• Make sure that chicken is bagged separately from other food products at the checkout counter of the grocery. Juices from the raw chicken should not touch other foods, such as lettuce or bakery products, which will not be cooked before eating.

• Keep uncooked chicken thoroughly chilled; leaving it at room temperature for any length of time will encourage salmonella growth. Uncooked chicken can be stored safely in the refrigerator for one to two days; most cooked chicken can be refrigerated up to four days after preparation. However, cooked ground chicken and chicken in

Microwave Magic

Defrosting in the microwave oven is a quick, safe way to thaw chicken. First, remove the chicken from the freezer wrapping, place in a microwave-safe dish, and cover. Microwave on Defrost or Medium Low (30% power) for 2 minutes. Let stand 2 minutes and repeat as needed until the chicken is thawed. Separate the chicken parts as they begin to thaw, and turn the chicken to prevent overcooking of particular areas.

gravy should be used within one to two days of preparation.

• Wash chicken thoroughly before cooking, and always use a clean knife and cutting board during preparation. Wash your hands, the knife, and the cutting board with hot, soapy water immediately after handling poultry to prevent cross-contamination with other foods.

• One of the safest places to thaw poultry is in the refrigerator. To safely thaw frozen chicken more quickly, place the wrapped package in a large bowl of cold water, and allow it to sit at room temperature 30 minutes. Change the water, and repeat this process until the chicken is thawed. Never leave a package of chicken sitting out on the counter to thaw because salmonella bacteria thrive at room temperature.

• Cook thawed chicken immediately, or refrigerate it until cooking time.

• Cooked chicken should be well done, never medium or rare. The most accurate way to determine whether chicken is done is to use a meat thermometer. Whole chicken should be cooked to an internal temperature of 180°F, while bone-in parts should be cooked to 170°F. Juice from the chicken should be clear when the meat is pierced with a fork.

• Do not place cooked chicken on the same platter that held the uncooked meat.

• Do not leave cooked chicken at room temperature for more than 2 hours. Cooked chicken should be kept either hot (140° to 165°F) or cold (below 40°F). Chicken salad is safe to take on a picnic as long as it is packed on ice and stored at or below 40°F during travel.

• Do not refrigerate or freeze a whole chicken or turkey with stuffing inside the cavity because of the risk of increased bacterial growth. Instead, store the meat and dressing separately.

IN THE KITCHEN

Here are some guidelines on freezing and preparing chicken at home.

• Properly packaged chicken parts can be frozen at 0°F for up to nine months, while a whole chicken will retain its quality up to one year. Giblets and ground chicken can be frozen for up to four months. For best results, remove the chicken from its packaging, rinse, and pat dry. Wrap the chicken tightly in heavy-duty plastic wrap or freezer paper before freezing. Remember to label and date.

• Chicken that has thawed should not be refrozen; quality can be affected.

• Most cooked poultry dishes can be frozen satisfactorily for four to six months. Cool in the refrigerator, and then wrap securely and freeze.

• Avoid freezing poultry dishes that contain either mayonnaise or hard-cooked egg because the mayonnaise tends to break down and the egg white becomes leathery.

• Most of the fat in poultry comes from the skin and pockets of fat just under the skin. You can remove the skin and cut away the excess fat before or after cooking.

If the recipe calls for boneless breast halves, but you have whole chicken breasts in the refrigerator, you can easily cut the chicken breast in half and remove the skin and bone. The only special equipment you will need is a knife with a thin, sharp blade.

1. Remove keel bone from the center of the chicken breast's underside.

2. Turn over breast, and using outline left by the keel bone as a guide, cut breast in half.

3. Carefully remove skin from the chicken breast halves.

4. Place cutting edge of knife toward bone. Using bone as a guide, separate meat from bone and rib cage.

CHICKEN COOKERY

Whether you simply need a cup of chopped cooked chicken or want to roast a whole broiler-fryer, here are the basic temperatures and times.

• *On the Cooktop:* Bring 1 cup water to a boil in a large skillet over medium-high heat. Reduce heat to simmer, and add 1 pound skinned, boned chicken breast halves. Cover skillet, and cook 15 minutes or until done, turning chicken after 8 minutes. (Seasonings such as herbs and pepper may be added to the cooking liquid, if desired.)

Cook a whole (3- to 3½-pound) broiler-fryer in boiling water to cover for 45 minutes to 1 hour or until tender. A 6-pound hen requires about 1½ hours cooking time.

• *In the Microwave:* Arrange 1 pound skinned, boned chicken breast halves in an 8-inch baking dish with thickest portions toward the outside of dish. Add ½ cup water and seasonings, if desired. Cover with heavy-duty plastic wrap, turning back one corner to vent. Microwave at HIGH 7 minutes or until juices run clear, rotating dish a quarter-turn after 4 minutes; let stand, covered, 3 minutes and drain.

• *On the Grill:* Place skinned, boned chicken breast halves (4 ounces each) between two sheets of heavy-duty plastic wrap; flatten each to ½-inch thickness using a meat mallet or rolling pin.

Marinate chicken in a low-fat commercial marinade, if desired. Place chicken on a grill rack coated with vegetable cooking spray. Grill chicken over medium-hot coals (350° to 400° F) for 6 minutes on each side or until done.

Grill bone-in breast halves (6 ounces each) for 8 to 10 minutes on each side or until done.

Cooking times will vary depending on the size of the chicken piece and the temperature of the fire. The most accurate test for doneness is to use a meat thermometer.

• *Under the Broiler:* Place skinned, boned chicken breast halves (4 ounces each) between 2 sheets of heavy-duty plastic wrap; flatten to ½-inch thickness using a meat mallet or rolling pin. Marinate chicken in a commercial low-fat marinade, if desired. Place chicken on the rack of a broiler pan coated with vegetable cooking spray. Broil 5½ inches from heat (with electric oven door partially opened) 5 to 6 minutes on each side or until done.

Broil bone-in breast halves (6 ounces each) for 8 to 10 minutes on each side on until chicken is done.

• *In the Oven:* Place a whole (3-pound) broiler-fryer on the rack of a broiler pan, and season with herbs or a commercial seasoning, if desired. Insert a meat thermometer into the meaty part of the thigh, making sure it does not touch the bone. Bake at 375° for 1½ hours or until meat thermometer registers 180° F.

A 2 to 3 pound chicken bakes in 1 to 1½ hours; a 3 to 4 pound chicken bakes in 1½ to 2 hours; and a 4 to 5 pound chicken bakes in 2 to 2½ hours. (Stuffed chickens require about 5 additional minutes per pound.)

A handy gadget for roasting a whole chicken is a vertical roasting rack which allows chicken to "stand-up" during roasting so that the fat drips into the roasting pan. It may be purchased at any kitchen shop.

To cook bone-in chicken pieces, place chicken in a baking pan, and bake at 350° for 1 hour or until chicken is done.

Chicken Hot Line

The United States Department of Agriculture (USDA) offers a toll-free hot line to answer questions on the safe storage, handling, and preparation of poultry and meat products. The number is (800) 535-4555. In Washington, D.C. dial 720-3333. The line is available on weekdays year-round from 10:00 a.m. to 4:00 p.m. eastern time, with extended hours during the month of November.

LOW-FAT BASICS

*W*hether you are trying to lose weight or not gain an extra pound, low-fat eating makes good sense. Research studies show that decreasing the amount of fat you eat reduces your risk of heart disease, diabetes, and some types of cancer. The goal recommended by major health groups is an intake of 30 percent or less of total daily calories.

Cooking Light Chicken Cookbook gives you practical, delicious recipes with realistic advice about low-fat cooking and eating. The recipes are lower in total fat than traditional recipes, and most provide less than 30 percent of calories from fat and less than 10 percent of calories from saturated fat.

The recommendation to reduce fat intake to no more than 30 percent of calories refers to fat intake for the entire day. If you have one higher fat item during a meal, you can balance it with lower-fat choices for the rest of the day and still remain within the recommended percentage.

For example, fat contributes 52 percent of the calories in Almond Cookies for the Ladies' Luncheon menu on page 25. However, because the cookies are combined with other low-fat foods, the total menu provides only 21 percent of calories as fat.

The goal of fat reduction need not be to eliminate all fat from your diet. In fact, some fat, although only a small amount, is needed to transport fat-soluble vitamins and maintain other normal body functions.

FIGURING THE FAT

The easiest way to achieve a diet with 30 percent or less of total calories from fat is to establish a daily fat budget according to your calorie level. Determine the total number of calories you eat or should eat each day based on your daily needs. To estimate your daily calorie requirements, multiply your current weight by 15. Remember that this is only a rough guide because calorie requirements vary according to age, body size, and level of activity. Add or subtract 500 calories a day to gain or lose 1 pound a week. (A diet of fewer than 1,200 calories a day is not recommended unless medically supervised.)

Once you arrive at your personal daily caloric requirement, it's easy to figure the number of fat grams you should consume each day. These should equal or be lower than the number of fat grams indicated on the Daily Fat Limits chart.

DAILY FAT LIMITS		
Calories Per Day	30 Percent of Calories	Grams of Fat
1,200	360	40
1,500	450	50
1,800	540	60
2,000	600	67
2,200	660	73
2,500	750	83
2,800	840	93

NUTRITIONAL ANALYSIS

Each recipe in *Cooking Light Chicken Cookbook* has been kitchen-tested by a staff of qualified home economists. Registered dietitians have determined the nutrient information using a computer system that analyzes every ingredient in any recipe. These efforts ensure the success of each recipe and will help you fit these recipes into your own meal planning.

Each recipe provides calories per serving and the percentage of calories from fat. A nutrient grid lists the grams of total fat, saturated fat, protein, and carbohydrate, and the milligrams of cholesterol and sodium per serving. The nutrient values are as accurate as possible and are based on these assumptions:

• When the recipe calls for cooked chicken, we base the analysis on chicken that has been skinned, trimmed of excess fat, and cooked without salt.

• Only the amount of marinade absorbed by the food is calculated.

• We do not include garnishes and optional ingredients in the analysis.

• Some of the alcohol calories evaporate during heating, and only those remaining are counted.

• When a range is given for an ingredient, we calculate the lesser amount.

SENSIBLE DINNERS

*W*hen it comes to menu planning, get smart. Use any of these menus as a guide to healthy eating. Each lists the total number of calories per serving and the percentage of calories that comes from fat. Once you catch on to the numbers game, you've learned a crucial low-fat lesson.

So take on the next challenge. Create a menu of your own by mixing and matching recipes. For example, Dinner on the Deck appeals if you serve Dijon-Glazed Chicken (page 134) instead of Sesame-Ginger Chicken (page 21).

(Of course, if you don't have time to play the numbers, you can always bet on these menus—all of them winners.)

Sweet Curry Chicken with Green Onion Rice (Recipes follow on page 19)

KIDS IN CHARGE

If your children want to join the kitchen patrol, let them have at it. There is no better time to introduce them to cooking. Just be sure to suggest a menu that will be both successful and fun. Each of these recipes is easy to prepare and suited for younger appetites, although adults will certainly enjoy them, too. Commercial dinner rolls can round out the menu. (One roll per serving is included in the analysis.)

Crispy Drumsticks

Broccoli-Pea Combo

Apple Salad with Maple Dressing

Commercial dinner rolls

Strawberry Sodas

Serves 4

TOTAL CALORIES PER SERVING: 496
(CALORIES FROM FAT: 15%)

Crispy Drumsticks with Broccoli-Pea Combo, Apple Salad, and Strawberry Soda

CRISPY DRUMSTICKS

¼ cup fine, dry breadcrumbs
⅛ teaspoon garlic powder
⅛ teaspoon onion powder
⅛ teaspoon dried whole marjoram
⅛ teaspoon dried whole thyme
1 egg white, lightly beaten
1 tablespoon skim milk
8 chicken drumsticks, skinned (about
    1½ pounds)
Vegetable cooking spray

Combine first 5 ingredients in a shallow dish; stir well. Combine egg white and milk in a small bowl. Dip each drumstick in milk mixture; dredge in breadcrumb mixture.

Place drumsticks in a 13- x 9- x 2-inch baking dish coated with cooking spray. Bake, uncovered, at 350° for 40 to 45 minutes or until done. Yield: 4 servings.

PER SERVING: 196 CALORIES (27% FROM FAT)
FAT 5.8G (SATURATED FAT 1.5G)
PROTEIN 28.7G CARBOHYDRATE 5.0G
CHOLESTEROL 89MG SODIUM 152MG

BROCCOLI-PEA COMBO

1½ cups frozen broccoli flowerets
1 cup frozen English peas
½ cup water
2 tablespoons chopped green onions
1 tablespoon diced pimiento
¼ teaspoon salt
¼ teaspoon dried whole dillweed

Combine first 4 ingredients in a medium saucepan; bring to a boil. Cover, reduce heat, and simmer 4 to 5 minutes or until crisp-tender. Drain vegetables. Stir in pimiento, salt, and dillweed. Yield: 4 servings.

PER SERVING: 40 CALORIES (7% FROM FAT)
FAT 0.3G (SATURATED FAT 0.0G)
PROTEIN 3.2G CARBOHYDRATE 7.1G
CHOLESTEROL 0MG SODIUM 191MG

APPLE SALAD WITH MAPLE DRESSING

3 tablespoons part-skim ricotta cheese
1 tablespoon plus 1 teaspoon reduced-calorie
    maple syrup
1 teaspoon skim milk
½ teaspoon vanilla extract
⅛ teaspoon ground cinnamon
4 lettuce leaves
2 cups coarsely chopped apple

Combine first 5 ingredients in container of an electric blender; cover and process until smooth. To serve, line salad plates with lettuce leaves. Spoon ½ cup apple onto each lettuce leaf; top with syrup mixture. Yield: 4 servings.

PER SERVING: 65 CALORIES (17% FROM FAT)
FAT 1.2G (SATURATED FAT 0.6G)
PROTEIN 1.8G CARBOHYDRATE 12.6G
CHOLESTEROL 4MG SODIUM 19MG

STRAWBERRY SODAS

2 cups strawberry nonfat ice cream
1 cup frozen unsweetened strawberries
½ cup skim milk
1 cup club soda, chilled

Combine strawberry ice cream, unsweetened strawberries, and skim milk in container of an electric blender; cover and process until strawberry mixture is smooth.

Add chilled club soda, stirring well to combine. Pour into glasses, and serve immediately. Yield: 4 (1-cup) servings.

PER SERVING: 129 CALORIES (1% FROM FAT)
FAT 0.1G (SATURATED FAT 0.0G)
PROTEIN 3.2G CARBOHYDRATE 28.3G
CHOLESTEROL 1MG SODIUM 74MG

Chicken Breasts Dijon with Zesty Broccoli and Rice Pilaf

COMPANY'S COMING

Need a meal in a hurry? With this menu, you can prepare dinner from start to finish in less than an hour. Serve your favorite flavor of sherbet for dessert (½ cup per serving), perhaps topped with fresh berries or other fruit.

Chicken Breasts Dijon

Zesty Broccoli

Rice Pilaf

Fruit sherbet

Serves 4
TOTAL CALORIES PER SERVING: 456
(CALORIES FROM FAT: 16%)

CHICKEN BREASTS DIJON

⅓ cup fine, dry breadcrumbs
1 tablespoon grated Parmesan cheese
½ teaspoon dried whole thyme
¼ teaspoon pepper
2 tablespoons creamy mustard-mayonnaise blend
4 (4-ounce) skinned, boned chicken breast halves
Vegetable cooking spray

Combine first 4 ingredients in a shallow dish; stir well, and set aside.

Brush mustard blend evenly over both sides of chicken. Dredge chicken in breadcrumb mixture.

Place chicken on a rack coated with cooking spray; place rack in shallow roasting pan. Bake at 375° for 45 minutes or until done. Yield: 4 servings.

PER SERVING: 174 CALORIES (14% FROM FAT)
FAT 2.8G (SATURATED FAT 0.7G)
PROTEIN 27.8G CARBOHYDRATE 6.8G
CHOLESTEROL 67MG SODIUM 381MG

ZESTY BROCCOLI

1 (16-ounce) package frozen broccoli spears
¼ cup commercial reduced-calorie Italian dressing
Lemon rind strips (optional)

Arrange broccoli in a vegetable steamer over boiling water. Cover and steam 8 minutes or until crisp-tender.

Place dressing in a 1-cup glass measure. Microwave at HIGH 1 minute or until hot, stirring after 30 seconds. Drizzle over broccoli. Garnish with lemon rind, if desired. Yield: 4 servings.

PER SERVING: 36 CALORIES (18% FROM FAT)
FAT 0.7G (SATURATED FAT 0.1G)
PROTEIN 3.2G CARBOHYDRATE 6.3G
CHOLESTEROL 0MG SODIUM 240MG

RICE PILAF

1 teaspoon olive oil
¾ cup chopped onion
2 tablespoons slivered almonds
1 cup long-grain rice, uncooked
¾ cup water
¼ teaspoon salt
⅛ teaspoon pepper
1 (13¾-ounce) can no-salt-added chicken broth
1 (2½-ounce) jar sliced mushrooms, drained
1 (2-ounce) jar diced pimiento, drained

Heat oil in a medium saucepan over medium-high heat. Add onion and almonds; sauté 5 minutes or until onion is tender and almonds are toasted. Add rice; sauté 1 minute. Add water and remaining ingredients; bring to a boil. Cover, reduce heat, and simmer 30 minutes or until liquid is absorbed.

Remove from heat, and let stand, covered, for 5 minutes. Yield: 4 servings.

PER SERVING: 114 CALORIES (23% FROM FAT)
FAT 2.9G (SATURATED FAT 0.3G)
PROTEIN 2.7G CARBOHYDRATE 19G
CHOLESTEROL 0MG SODIUM 226MG

A NEIGHBORLY SUPPER

Give a warm welcome to your neighbors with easy-to-prepare curry-flavored chicken sauté. Toss together an assortment of greens for the salad (1 cup per serving). Minimize fat and calories by offering chocolate frozen yogurt (½ cup each) for dessert.

Sweet Curry Chicken

Green Onion Rice

Salad greens with Fresh Herb Dressing

Chocolate frozen yogurt

Serves 6
TOTAL CALORIES PER SERVING: 489
(CALORIES FROM FAT: 18%)

Sweet Curry Chicken

SWEET CURRY CHICKEN
(pictured on page 12)

1 (20-ounce) can unsweetened pineapple
   tidbits
¼ cup unsweetened orange juice
¼ cup unsweetened pineapple juice
1 tablespoon cornstarch
1¾ teaspoons curry powder
2 teaspoons honey
3 tablespoons all-purpose flour
½ teaspoon crushed red pepper flakes
1½ pounds skinned, boned chicken breasts,
   cut into 1-inch cubes
Vegetable cooking spray
1 tablespoon corn oil
1 medium-size green pepper, cut into ¼-inch-
   wide strips
1 medium-size sweet red or yellow pepper, cut
   into ¼-inch-wide strips
½ teaspoon salt

Drain pineapple tidbits, reserving the juice. Set pineapple tidbits aside.

Combine the reserved pineapple juice, orange juice, ¼ cup additional pineapple juice, cornstarch, curry powder, and honey in a heavy saucepan. Bring to a boil, stirring constantly. Reduce heat; simmer 3 to 4 minutes or until thickened. Set mixture aside.

Place flour and crushed red pepper flakes in a zip-top plastic bag. Add chicken, and shake to coat lightly. Coat a large skillet with cooking spray; add oil, and place over medium heat until hot. Add chicken, and sauté 6 to 8 minutes or until chicken is lightly browned and tender. Remove chicken from skillet; wipe skillet with paper towels.

Coat skillet with cooking spray. Add pepper strips, and sauté until crisp-tender. Add cooked chicken, reserved pineapple tidbits, salt, and reserved curry sauce mixture. Cook over medium heat until thoroughly heated. Yield: 6 servings.

PER SERVING: 257 CALORIES (15% FROM FAT)
FAT 4.3G (SATURATED FAT 0.7G)
PROTEIN 27.2G CARBOHYDRATE 26.2G
CHOLESTEROL 66MG SODIUM 273MG

GREEN ONION RICE
(pictured on page 12)

Vegetable cooking spray
2¾ cups cooked long-grain rice (cooked
   without salt or fat)
½ cup chopped green onions
¼ teaspoon curry powder
¼ teaspoon ground cumin
¼ teaspoon freshly ground black pepper

Coat a large skillet with vegetable cooking spray, and place over medium-high heat until hot. Add rice, green onions, curry powder, cumin, and pepper; sauté 3 to 5 minutes or until thoroughly heated. Yield: 6 servings.

PER SERVING: 103 CALORIES (2% FROM FAT)
FAT 0.2G (SATURATED FAT 0.0G)
PROTEIN 2.0G CARBOHYDRATE 22.7G
CHOLESTEROL 0MG SODIUM 2MG

FRESH HERB DRESSING

½ cup tarragon vinegar
¼ cup chopped fresh parsley
3½ tablespoons water
2 tablespoons chopped fresh chives
1 teaspoon sugar
1 teaspoon chopped fresh tarragon
2 teaspoons olive oil
½ teaspoon freshly ground pepper

Combine all ingredients in a small jar; cover tightly, and shake vigorously to blend. Chill thoroughly. Serve with salad greens. Yield: ¾ cup.

PER TABLESPOON: 14 CALORIES (51% FROM FAT)
FAT 0.8G (SATURATED FAT 0.1G)
PROTEIN 0.6G CARBOHYDRATE 1.4G
CHOLESTEROL 0MG SODIUM 2MG

Sesame-Ginger Chicken, Grilled Vegetable Kabob, and toasted French bread

DINNER ON THE DECK

With soft breezes heralding warm weather, move the kitchen outdoors. You can cook this menu almost completely on the grill. First, prepare the raspberry puree, and allow it to chill. Next, assemble the kabobs, and start the rice. While the kabobs cook, prepare the chicken and peaches for the grill. Place ½-inch slices of French bread on the grill, allowing one slice per person, and toast until golden. Mix the cooler just before serving.

Fruit Juice Cooler

Sesame-Ginger Chicken

Grilled Vegetable Kabobs with Rice

Toasted French bread

Grilled Peaches with Raspberry Puree

Serves 4
TOTAL CALORIES PER SERVING: 596
(CALORIES FROM FAT: 10%)

FRUIT JUICE COOLER

2 (6½-ounce) bottles sparkling mineral water, chilled
1 (12-ounce) can peach nectar, chilled
½ cup unsweetened orange juice, chilled
¼ cup unsweetened grapefruit juice, chilled
2 tablespoons lemon juice, chilled

Combine all ingredients in a large pitcher; mix well. Serve immediately. Yield: 4 (1-cup) servings.

PER SERVING: 68 CALORIES (3% FROM FAT)
FAT 0.2G (SATURATED FAT 0G)
PROTEIN 0.5G CARBOHYDRATE 17.2G
CHOLESTEROL 0MG SODIUM 26MG

Calorie Countdown

A low-fat diet and regular exercise are key in losing or maintaining weight. Women should generally eat 1,200 to 1,600 calories daily when trying to lose weight, while most men may consume 1,600 to 2,000 calories.

SESAME-GINGER CHICKEN

1 tablespoon sesame seeds, toasted
2 tablespoons honey
2 tablespoons reduced-sodium soy sauce
2 teaspoons peeled, grated gingerroot
4 (4-ounce) skinned, boned chicken breast halves
Vegetable cooking spray
Thin green onion strips (optional)

Combine first 4 ingredients in a small bowl; stir well, and set aside.

Place chicken between 2 sheets of heavy-duty plastic wrap, and flatten to ¼-inch thickness, using a meat mallet or rolling pin.

Coat grill rack with cooking spray; place on grill over medium-hot coals. Place chicken on rack; grill 4 to 5 minutes on each side or until done, basting frequently with soy sauce mixture. Transfer chicken to a serving platter; garnish with green onion strips, if desired. Yield: 4 servings.

PER SERVING: 186 CALORIES (20% FROM FAT)
FAT 4.2G (SATURATED FAT 1.0G)
PROTEIN 26.6G CARBOHYDRATE 9.7G
CHOLESTEROL 70MG SODIUM 304MG

GRILLED VEGETABLE KABOBS WITH RICE

½ cup commercial oil-free Italian dressing
1 tablespoon minced fresh parsley or 1
    teaspoon dried parsley flakes
1 teaspoon dried whole basil
2 medium-size yellow squash, cut into 1-inch
    slices
8 small boiling onions
8 cherry tomatoes
8 medium-size fresh mushrooms
Vegetable cooking spray
2 cups cooked long-grain rice (cooked without
    salt or fat)

Combine dressing, parsley, and basil in a small bowl; cover and chill.

Alternate squash, onions, tomatoes, and mushrooms on 8 skewers. Coat grill rack with cooking spray; place on grill over medium coals. Place kabobs on rack, and cook 15 minutes or until vegetables are tender, turning and basting frequently with dressing mixture.

To serve, place ½ cup rice on each plate, and top with 2 vegetable kabobs. Yield: 4 servings.

PER SERVING: 184 CALORIES (4% FROM FAT)
FAT 0.8G (SATURATED FAT 0.1G)
PROTEIN 4.9G CARBOHYDRATE 40.5G
CHOLESTEROL 0MG SODIUM 331MG

GRILLED PEACHES WITH RASPBERRY PUREE

½ (10-ounce) package frozen raspberries in
    light syrup, slightly thawed
1½ teaspoons lemon juice
2 medium peaches, peeled, halved, and pitted
1½ tablespoons brown sugar
¼ teaspoon ground cinnamon
1½ teaspoons rum flavoring
1½ teaspoons margarine

Combine raspberries and lemon juice in container of an electric blender or food processor; cover and process until smooth. Strain raspberry puree; discard seeds. Cover and chill.

Cut 1 (18- x 18-inch) sheet of heavy-duty aluminum foil. Place peach halves, cut side up, on foil. Combine brown sugar and cinnamon; spoon evenly into center of each peach half.

Sprinkle with rum flavoring, and dot with margarine. Fold foil over peaches, and loosely seal.

Place grill rack over medium coals; place peach bundle on rack, and cook 15 minutes or until peaches are thoroughly heated.

To serve, spoon 2 tablespoons raspberry puree over each grilled peach half. Yield: 4 servings.

PER SERVING: 89 CALORIES (15% FROM FAT)
FAT 1.5G (SATURATED FAT 0.3G)
PROTEIN 0.6G CARBOHYDRATE 17.7G
CHOLESTEROL 0MG SODIUM 18MG

Fat Burner

A healthy lifestyle includes a variety of foods in moderation every day. However, if you want to lose weight, try the following:

• Eat foods high in fat less often than low-fat foods. Fat is twice as dense in calories as carbohydrates and protein.

• Be aware of portion sizes. Each of our recipes states the appropriate number of servings.

• Take a long-lasting approach to weight loss by changing eating habits permanently, not just crash dieting in order to fit into that new swimsuit by summer.

• Avoid faddish weight-loss diets that promote one food or nutrient.

• Work up a sweat! Dieters who exercise are more likely to keep fat off than sedentary people.

LADIES' LUNCHEON

Everyone loves a themed menu. Look to the Orient to inspire your next get-together. Best of all, it's a no-fuss affair. Prepare the cookies and tea the day before and the chicken salad and soup on the day of your luncheon. Balance the meal with rice cakes, allowing two per guest. The analysis also includes two Almond Cookies per serving.

Orange-Ginger Tea

Egg Drop Soup

Oriental Chicken Salad

Commercial miniature rice cakes

Almond Cookies

Serves 4
TOTAL CALORIES PER SERVING: 419
(CALORIES FROM FAT: 21%)

ORANGE-GINGER TEA

4¼ cups water
1 (2-inch) piece peeled, sliced gingerroot
4 regular-size tea bags
3 tablespoons sugar
2 teaspoons orange extract
½ teaspoon ground ginger

Combine water and sliced gingerroot in a saucepan; bring to a boil. Pour boiling ginger mixture over tea bags; steep 5 minutes. Strain tea; discard ginger and tea bags. Stir in sugar, orange extract, and ground ginger. Serve warm or chilled over ice. Yield: 4 (1-cup) servings.

PER SERVING: 56 CALORIES (2% FROM FAT)
FAT 0.1G (SATURATED FAT 0G)
PROTEIN 0.2G   CARBOHYDRATE 11.1G
CHOLESTEROL 0MG   SODIUM 2MG

EGG DROP SOUP

2 cups canned low-sodium chicken broth, undiluted
1½ cups water
1 tablespoon low-sodium soy sauce
¼ cup canned, sliced mushrooms, drained
1 tablespoon plus 1 teaspoon cornstarch
2 tablespoons dry sherry
1 egg
1 egg white, lightly beaten
¼ cup thinly sliced green onions

Combine first 3 ingredients in a saucepan; bring to a boil. Add mushrooms.

Combine cornstarch and sherry; add to broth mixture. Cook 1 minute over medium heat; stir constantly. Combine egg and egg white. Slowly pour egg mixture into boiling broth mixture, stirring constantly.

Ladle soup into bowls; sprinkle each serving with 1 tablespoon onions. Yield: 4 (1-cup) servings.

PER SERVING: 51 CALORIES (23% FROM FAT)
FAT 1.3G (SATURATED FAT 0.4G)
PROTEIN 3.2G   CARBOHYDRATE 4.7G
CHOLESTEROL 55MG   SODIUM 197MG

Clockwise from top: *Egg Drop Soup, Orange-Ginger Tea, and Oriental Chicken Salad*

ORIENTAL CHICKEN SALAD

½ pound skinned, boned chicken breasts
1 (10-ounce) package frozen broccoli flowerets, thawed
½ cup sliced water chestnuts
½ cup mandarin oranges in light syrup, drained
⅓ cup unsweetened orange juice
3 tablespoons cider vinegar
1 tablespoon low-sodium soy sauce
2 teaspoons sugar
1½ teaspoons dark sesame oil
1 teaspoon grated orange rind
¼ teaspoon salt
¼ teaspoon ground ginger
⅛ teaspoon crushed red pepper
4 cups shredded Napa cabbage
2 tablespoons chow mein noodles
1 tablespoon sesame seeds, toasted

Place chicken in a nonstick skillet; cover with water. Bring to a boil; cover, reduce heat, and simmer 15 minutes or until done. Cut into strips.

Combine chicken, broccoli, water chestnuts, and mandarin oranges.

Combine orange juice and next 8 ingredients. Pour juice mixture over chicken mixture; toss gently. Arrange 1 cup cabbage on each of 4 serving plates. Top with chicken mixture; sprinkle with noodles and sesame seeds. Yield: 4 servings.

PER SERVING: 183 CALORIES (21% FROM FAT)
FAT 4.3G (SATURATED FAT 0.7G)
PROTEIN 16.9G CARBOHYDRATE 20.2G
CHOLESTEROL 33MG SODIUM 350MG

ALMOND COOKIES

¼ cup plus 2 tablespoons margarine, softened
¼ cup sugar
1 egg yolk
½ teaspoon almond extract
¼ teaspoon lemon extract
¼ teaspoon vanilla extract
1 cup all-purpose flour
½ teaspoon baking powder
Dash of salt
24 almond slices (about 1 tablespoon)

Cream margarine; gradually add sugar, beating at medium speed of an electric mixer until light and fluffy. Add egg yolk and extracts; beat well.

Combine flour, baking powder, and salt; add to creamed mixture, beating well.

Shape dough into 1-inch balls. Place 2 inches apart on ungreased cookie sheets. Press an almond slice in center of each cookie. Bake at 350° for 6 to 8 minutes or until lightly browned. Remove from cookie sheets, and let cool on wire racks. Yield: 2 dozen cookies.

PER COOKIE: 59 CALORIES (52% FROM FAT)
FAT 3.4G (SATURATED FAT 0.7G)
PROTEIN 0.8G CARBOHYDRATE 6.3G
CHOLESTEROL 9MG SODIUM 40MG

FYI

Cookies that provide 52 percent of calories as fat? Indulge—and don't ask permission! This menu lets you "sneak" a little without really cheating. Simple explanation: The other foods in the menu all fall below the 30 percent fat level. When the menu is looked at as a whole, the average fat content is only 21 percent. A balanced menu will always "outweigh" one small transgression.

SNACKS & SANDWICHES

*T*hink of the sandwich as an old standby? The kind your mom slapped together on Saturday afternoon? No more. Discover the secret to sandwich success: chicken—that taken-for-granted item you toss in the grocery cart each week. But check the ho-hum at the register. Prepared with a little imagination, chicken takes top honors as a versatile sandwich filling or a favorite snack. You can serve chicken any day of the week and for any type of meal—whether you're brown-bagging, tossing together snacks, whipping up appetizers, or spiffing up a luncheon. As for variety, you'll find recipes for almost any occasion in this collection.

Spicy Chicken Pockets (Recipe follows on page 35)

THAI POT STICKERS

Vegetable cooking spray
½ teaspoon vegetable oil
1 tablespoon peeled, minced gingerroot
1 tablespoon minced garlic
¾ cup finely shredded cooked chicken breast
¼ cup minced water chestnuts
2 tablespoons minced fresh cilantro
1 tablespoon minced fresh mint
1 teaspoon sesame seeds, lightly toasted
½ teaspoon ground cumin
⅛ teaspoon salt
8 egg roll wrappers
1 tablespoon water
1 tablespoon vegetable oil
⅔ cup water
¼ cup no-sugar-added apricot spread
⅓ cup reduced-sodium teriyaki sauce
1 tablespoon hot sauce
1 tablespoon lime juice

Coat a large nonstick skillet with cooking spray; add ½ teaspoon oil. Place over medium-high heat until hot. Add gingerroot and garlic; cook, stirring constantly, until tender. Remove from heat, and stir in chicken and next 6 ingredients.

Cut egg roll wrappers in half lengthwise. Lightly brush edges with 1 tablespoon water. Place about 1 tablespoon chicken mixture at base of a wrapper half; fold the right bottom corner over to form a triangle. Continue folding back and forth into a triangle to end of wrapper half. Repeat procedure with remaining wrapper halves and chicken mixture.

Coat a large skillet with cooking spray; add 1 tablespoon oil. Add filled egg roll wrappers; cook over medium-high heat 1 minute on each side or until golden. Add ⅔ cup water; cook 5 minutes or until water evaporates, turning once.

Combine apricot spread and remaining ingredients; stir well. Serve pot stickers with apricot sauce. Yield: 16 appetizers.

PER APPETIZER: 53 CALORIES (29% FROM FAT)
FAT 1.7G (SATURATED FAT 0.4G)
PROTEIN 3.7G CARBOHYDRATE 5.4G
CHOLESTEROL 19MG SODIUM 158MG

CHICKEN NACHO DIP

Keep the fat low with this appetizer dip by serving it with no-oil baked tortilla chips instead of regular corn chips.

1 (1¼-ounce) package taco seasoning mix
2½ cups shredded cooked chicken breast
½ cup light beer
1 (4-ounce) can chopped green chiles, undrained
½ cup commercial no-salt-added salsa
1 (15-ounce) can black beans, drained
1 tablespoon crushed garlic
½ cup minced fresh cilantro
1½ cups (6 ounces) shredded fat-free Cheddar cheese
1 (16-ounce) carton nonfat sour cream alternative
1½ cups seeded, diced tomato
½ cup minced green onions
¼ cup sliced ripe olives

Reserve 1 teaspoon taco seasoning mix; set aside. Combine remaining taco seasoning mix, chicken, beer, and chiles in a large skillet; bring to a boil. Reduce heat, and simmer, uncovered, 5 minutes or until mixture is thickened. Remove from heat; stir in salsa.

Mash beans and garlic until smooth; stir in cilantro. Spread bean mixture in a 10-inch quiche dish. Spoon chicken mixture evenly over bean mixture; top with cheese. Bake, uncovered, at 375° for 15 minutes or until cheese melts and mixture is thoroughly heated.

Combine sour cream and reserved taco seasoning mix; spread over melted cheese. Top with tomato, green onions, and olives. Serve with no-oil baked tortilla chips. Yield: 30 appetizers.

PER APPETIZER: 69 CALORIES (18% FROM FAT)
FAT 1.4G (SATURATED FAT 0.3G)
PROTEIN 8.1G CARBOHYDRATE 5.6G
CHOLESTEROL 14MG SODIUM 186MG

HONEY-MUSTARD CHICKEN NUGGETS

¼ cup honey
2 tablespoons prepared mustard
1 tablespoon reduced-calorie margarine
2 teaspoons low-sodium soy sauce
½ pound skinned, boned chicken breasts, cut into 18 (1-inch) pieces
½ cup cornflake crumbs
1 teaspoon paprika

Combine first 4 ingredients in a microwave-safe medium bowl; stir well, and microwave at HIGH 20 seconds or until margarine melts. Add chicken pieces, stirring to coat.

Combine cornflake crumbs and paprika; dredge each chicken piece in cornflake crumb mixture, using wooden picks.

Arrange half of chicken pieces in a circle around the edge of a large, heavy-duty paper plate; cover with wax paper, and microwave at HIGH 2 to 2½ minutes. Repeat procedure with remaining chicken pieces.

Microwave remaining honey-mustard sauce at HIGH 1 to 1½ minutes or until hot. Serve with chicken nuggets. Yield: 6 appetizer servings.

Note: Chicken may be baked, if desired. Place on a baking sheet coated with cooking spray; bake at 400° for 15 minutes or until chicken is done.

PER SERVING: 136 CALORIES (13% FROM FAT)
FAT 2.0G (SATURATED FAT 0.1G)
PROTEIN 9.7G   CARBOHYDRATE 20.4G
CHOLESTEROL 22MG   SODIUM 245MG

Honey-Mustard Chicken Nuggets

CHICKEN CURRY IN PHYLLO BASKETS

1 (8-ounce) carton plain nonfat yogurt
5 sheets commercial frozen phyllo pastry, thawed
Vegetable cooking spray
1½ cups finely diced, skinned smoked chicken breast
½ cup minced sweet red pepper
2 tablespoons finely chopped pecans, toasted
2 tablespoons minced green onions
2 teaspoons curry powder
⅛ teaspoon salt

Use a yogurt cheesemaker or line a colander with 4 layers of cheesecloth, allowing cheesecloth to extend over edge of colander; place in a glass bowl. Spoon yogurt into cheesemaker or colander; cover with plastic wrap. Refrigerate yogurt at least 8 hours.

Place 1 sheet phyllo on a damp towel (keep remaining phyllo covered). Lightly coat phyllo with cooking spray. Layer remaining 4 sheets phyllo on first sheet, lightly coating each sheet with cooking spray. Cut phyllo stack into 28 rounds, using a 2½-inch biscuit cutter, and discard remaining phyllo.

Place a phyllo round into each of 28 miniature (1¾-inch) muffin cups coated with cooking spray. Press phyllo rounds against the bottom and up the sides of each cup. Bake at 350° for 8 minutes or until golden; let cool completely in pans. Transfer to a serving platter.

Spoon drained yogurt into a bowl; discard liquid. Add chicken and next 5 ingredients; stir well. Cover and refrigerate up to 3 hours. Just before serving, spoon chicken mixture evenly into phyllo cups. Yield: 28 appetizers.

PER APPETIZER: 37 CALORIES (29% FROM FAT)
FAT 1.2G (SATURATED FAT 0.2G)
PROTEIN 3.4G   CARBOHYDRATE 3.4G
CHOLESTEROL 6MG   SODIUM 86MG

ROMAINE-WRAPPED GINGER CHICKEN

9 large romaine lettuce leaves
¼ cup canned no-salt-added chicken broth, undiluted
1 tablespoon dry sherry
1 tablespoon low-sodium soy sauce
1½ teaspoons cornstarch
¼ teaspoon dark sesame oil
Dash of ground red pepper
1 (10-ounce) package frozen chopped turnip greens, cooked without salt
Vegetable cooking spray
½ teaspoon vegetable oil
1½ teaspoons peeled, grated gingerroot
1 small clove garlic, minced
Dash of ground red pepper
¾ cup chopped fresh mushrooms
½ cup coarsely chopped sweet red pepper
½ cup finely chopped canned water chestnuts
6 ounces skinned, boned chicken breast, cut into ½-inch cubes

Cut off raised portion of the main vein of each lettuce leaf. Plunge leaves into boiling water, and cook 10 seconds; drain and rinse under cold running water. Set aside. Combine chicken broth and next 5 ingredients. Stir well, and set aside.

Drain turnip greens well. Place on paper towels, and squeeze until barely moist; set aside.

Coat a large saucepan with cooking spray. Add oil, and place over medium-high heat until hot. Add next 3 ingredients; sauté 30 seconds. Add turnip greens, mushrooms, and sweet red pepper; sauté 1 minute. Add water chestnuts and chicken; sauté 1 minute. Add chicken broth mixture; bring to a boil. Cook, stirring constantly, 2 minutes or until mixture is thickened and chicken is done.

Spoon ¼ cup chicken mixture onto lower third of each lettuce leaf. Fold sides in, and roll up, starting at stem end. Serve warm. Yield: 9 appetizers.

PER APPETIZER: 49 CALORIES (17% FROM FAT)
FAT 0.9G (SATURATED FAT 0.2G)
PROTEIN 5.5G   CARBOHYDRATE 4.9G
CHOLESTEROL 11MG   SODIUM 83MG

Romaine-Wrapped Ginger Chicken

HONEY-MUSTARD GLAZED MEATBALLS

¼ cup honey
½ teaspoon grated lemon rind
2 tablespoons low-sodium soy sauce
1 tablespoon Dijon mustard
1 tablespoon fresh lemon juice
Vegetable cooking spray
2 teaspoons vegetable oil
1 cup finely chopped onion
1 cup finely chopped green pepper
2 cloves garlic, minced
1½ pounds freshly ground raw chicken thighs
½ cup fine, dry breadcrumbs
½ cup coarsely shredded zucchini
½ teaspoon salt
½ teaspoon grated lemon rind
¼ teaspoon pepper
2 teaspoons Dijon mustard
2 teaspoons fresh lemon juice
1 teaspoon low-sodium soy sauce

Combine first 5 ingredients; stir well with a wire whisk, and set aside.

Coat a large nonstick skillet with cooking spray; add oil, and place over medium heat until hot. Add onion, green pepper, and garlic, and sauté 5 minutes or until tender. Let onion mixture cool.

Combine onion mixture, chicken, and next 8 ingredients in a bowl; stir well. Shape mixture into 48 (1¼-inch) balls. Recoat skillet with cooking spray, and place over medium heat until hot.

Add half of meatballs; cook 15 minutes or until browned, turning frequently. Remove from skillet, and keep warm; repeat with remaining meatballs. Return cooked meatballs to skillet. Pour honey mixture over meatballs; cook 3 minutes or until sauce is thickened, stirring constantly. Yield: 4 dozen appetizers.

PER APPETIZER: 32 CALORIES (25% FROM FAT)
FAT 0.9G (SATURATED FAT 0.2G)
PROTEIN 3.1G   CARBOHYDRATE 2.9G
CHOLESTEROL 12MG   SODIUM 84MG

CHICKEN PÂTÉ SANDWICHES

These appetizer sandwiches are great for a cocktail buffet. The spread can be prepared and chilled the day before; on party day assemble the sandwiches, and store them according to the note below.

2 cups water
1 (4-ounce) skinned, boned chicken breast half
2½ tablespoons reduced-calorie mayonnaise
1½ tablespoons commercial mango chutney
⅛ teaspoon pepper
7 (½-ounce) slices very thin white or wheat bread
7 cherry tomatoes, halved and cut into quarters
14 tiny sprigs fresh parsley

Bring water to a boil in a saucepan. Reduce heat, and add chicken; cover and simmer 13 minutes or until tender. Drain and let cool.

Position knife blade in food processor bowl; add chicken. Process until finely chopped. Add mayonnaise, chutney, and pepper; process until well blended. Set aside.

Trim crusts from bread; discard crusts. Spread about 4 teaspoons chicken mixture over each slice. Cut each slice in half to make 2 rectangles. Top with tomatoes and parsley. Yield: 7 servings.

Note: To store, place sandwiches on a serving platter. Cover with a slightly damp paper towel and plastic wrap. Refrigerate until ready to serve.

PER SERVING: 74 CALORIES (28% FROM FAT)
FAT 2.3G (SATURATED FAT 0.4G)
PROTEIN 5.2G   CARBOHYDRATE 8.7G
CHOLESTEROL 12MG   SODIUM 117MG

Chicken Pâté Sandwiches

ORIENTAL CHICKEN PITAS

1½ cups chopped cooked chicken breast
1 cup alfalfa sprouts
½ cup chopped water chestnuts
½ cup sliced green onions
2 tablespoons rice wine vinegar
2 tablespoons reduced-sodium soy sauce
2 teaspoons dark sesame oil
2 (6-inch) whole wheat pita bread rounds, cut in half crosswise
4 lettuce leaves

Combine first 4 ingredients in a large bowl. Combine vinegar, soy sauce, and sesame oil; pour over chicken mixture, and toss gently. Line pita halves with lettuce. Spoon chicken mixture evenly into pita halves. Yield: 4 servings.

PER SERVING: 223 CALORIES (21% FROM FAT)
FAT 5.2G (SATURATED FAT 1.1G)
PROTEIN 23.4G CARBOHYDRATE 18.7G
CHOLESTEROL 57MG SODIUM 730MG

Menu Helper

The pocket in a pita bread round makes an ideal container for fillings that tend to "fall out" of ordinary sandwich breads. Both white and whole wheat pita breads are available, are relatively low in fat and calories, and make ordinary sandwich fillings more interesting. French bread, sourdough rolls, Italian bread, tortillas, or English muffins also work well.

TANDOORI CHICKEN TIKAS

Tikas is the Indian word for "tidbits." In this recipe, bite-size chicken pieces are highly seasoned with curry and pepper. You may wish to cut back on the seasonings if the dish is too spicy for your taste.

⅔ cup plain low-fat yogurt
3 tablespoons paprika
2 tablespoons curry powder
2 teaspoons freshly ground pepper
1 teaspoon white vinegar
¾ teaspoon peeled, grated gingerroot
¼ teaspoon salt
2 cloves garlic, crushed
1 pound skinned, boned chicken breast, cut into 24 bite-size pieces
Vegetable cooking spray
2 (6-inch) pita bread rounds, cut in half crosswise
½ cup plain low-fat yogurt

Combine first 8 ingredients in a medium bowl, and stir well. Add chicken to yogurt mixture; stir well. Cover and marinate 8 hours. Remove chicken from marinade, reserving marinade. Thread 6 chicken pieces onto each of 4 (8-inch) skewers.
Place skewers on a broiler rack coated with cooking spray, and place rack on a broiler pan. Broil 5½ inches from heat (with electric oven door partially opened) 6 minutes. Turn skewers over; brush with reserved marinade. Broil an additional 6 minutes or until chicken is done; remove chicken from skewers. Fill each pita half with 6 chicken pieces, and top with 2 tablespoons yogurt. Yield: 4 servings.

PER SERVING: 271 CALORIES (20% FROM FAT)
FAT 6.0G (SATURATED FAT 1.8G)
PROTEIN 33.1G CARBOHYDRATE 21.4G
CHOLESTEROL 77MG SODIUM 368MG

SPICY CHICKEN POCKETS
(pictured on page 26)

1½ pounds skinned, boned chicken breasts
Spicy Creole Seasoning Blend
Vegetable cooking spray
2 tablespoons corn oil
4 (7-inch) whole-wheat pita bread rounds, cut
   in half crosswise
8 leaf lettuce leaves
1 small red onion, thinly sliced and separated
   into rings
1 cup alfalfa sprouts
¾ cup diced cucumber
¾ cup chopped tomato
Zesty Yogurt Dressing

Rub chicken with Spicy Creole Seasoning Blend, and place in a large, shallow dish. Cover and refrigerate at least 30 minutes.

Coat grill rack with cooking spray; place on grill over medium-hot coals (350° to 400°). Brush both sides of chicken with oil. Place chicken on grill rack; grill 5 to 6 minutes on each side or until chicken is done. Remove from grill; set aside.

Line each pita half with a lettuce leaf. Layer onion, alfalfa sprouts, cucumber, and tomato evenly into each pita half. Cut chicken into strips, and arrange evenly over layered vegetables. Drizzle Zesty Yogurt Dressing evenly into each pita half. Yield: 8 servings.

Note: To broil chicken, coat the rack of a broiler pan with cooking spray. Place chicken on rack, and broil 5½ inches from heat (with electric oven door partially opened) 5 to 6 minutes on each side or until chicken is done.

PER SERVING: 257 CALORIES (23% FROM FAT)
FAT 6.7G (SATURATED FAT 1.1G)
PROTEIN 23.0G CARBOHYDRATE 24.2G
CHOLESTEROL 53MG SODIUM 380MG

SPICY CREOLE SEASONING BLEND
1 tablespoon paprika
2 teaspoons dried whole thyme, crushed
2 teaspoons garlic powder
2 teaspoons onion powder
1 teaspoon ground red pepper
½ teaspoon salt
½ teaspoon dry mustard
¼ teaspoon freshly ground black pepper

Combine paprika, thyme, garlic powder, onion powder, red pepper, salt, dry mustard, and black pepper in a small bowl; stir well. Seasoning blend may be stored in a zip-top plastic bag until ready to use. Yield: about ¼ cup.

ZESTY YOGURT DRESSING
½ cup plain nonfat yogurt
1 tablespoon minced fresh parsley
1 tablespoon skim milk
1 tablespoon lemon juice
2 teaspoons sugar
1 teaspoon honey mustard
Dash of hot sauce

Combine all ingredients in a small bowl; stir well. Cover and refrigerate. Yield: ¾ cup.

Note: Zesty Yogurt Dressing may be made up to 3 days ahead. Refrigerate until ready to use.

The secret to delicious grilled chicken is proper temperature of the coals, correct placement of the grill rack, and adequate cooking time. The rack should be placed about 6 inches above medium-hot coals. Skinned, boned breast halves cook very quickly and will toughen and become dry if overcooked.

BLACKENED CHICKEN PITAS

Leaf lettuce is recommended here, but any that you have on hand will do. Shredded spinach leaves are another option.

½ teaspoon salt
¼ teaspoon paprika
¼ teaspoon ground red pepper
¼ teaspoon black pepper
⅛ teaspoon garlic powder
⅛ teaspoon onion powder
⅛ teaspoon ground cumin
1 tablespoon plus 1 teaspoon margarine, divided
4 (4-ounce) skinned, boned chicken breast halves
1 cup vertically sliced onion
2 (6-inch) pita bread rounds, cut in half crosswise
2 cups loosely packed shredded leaf lettuce
4 (¼-inch-thick) slices unpeeled tomato, cut in half (about 1 small)

Combine first 7 ingredients in a bowl; rub over chicken. Place a skillet over high heat until hot; add 1 tablespoon margarine, and quickly tilt in all directions so margarine covers bottom. Add chicken; cook 2 minutes on each side or until blackened and charred. Remove chicken.

Melt remaining 1 teaspoon margarine in skillet over medium-high heat; add onion, and sauté 1 minute. Reduce heat to medium, and cook 5 minutes or until tender, stirring occasionally. Line each pita half with ½ cup shredded lettuce. Arrange 1 piece chicken and 2 tomato pieces over lettuce in each pita; top with onion mixture. Yield: 4 servings.

PER SERVING: 259 CALORIES (30% FROM FAT)
FAT 8.5G (SATURATED FAT 2.0G)
PROTEIN 28.9G CARBOHYDRATE 15.3G
CHOLESTEROL 73MG SODIUM 515MG

INDONESIAN PITAS

2 tablespoons brown sugar
1 tablespoon chopped onion
2 tablespoons chunky peanut butter
2 tablespoons 62%-less-sodium soy sauce
1 tablespoon lemon juice
¾ cup canned low-sodium chicken broth, undiluted
1 clove garlic, minced
¼ teaspoon ground red pepper
1 pound skinned, boned chicken breasts, cut into ¼-inch strips
Vegetable cooking spray
2 (6-inch) pita bread rounds, cut in half crosswise
24 (⅛-inch-thick) slices peeled cucumber

Combine first 7 ingredients in a bowl; stir well, and set aside.

Sprinkle pepper over chicken. Coat a nonstick skillet with cooking spray; place over high heat until hot. Add chicken; stir-fry 4 minutes or until browned. Remove chicken; set aside. Add peanut butter mixture to skillet; cook 3 minutes or until thickened, stirring constantly. Return chicken to skillet; cook 30 seconds or until heated. Spoon ½ cup chicken mixture into each pita half; top with 6 cucumber slices. Yield: 4 servings.

PER SERVING: 264 CALORIES (23% FROM FAT)
FAT 6.6G (SATURATED FAT 1.4G)
PROTEIN 31.0G CARBOHYDRATE 18.6G
CHOLESTEROL 67MG SODIUM 432MG

Menu Helper

Combine any of our pita sandwiches with hot soup, and you've got a great cold-weather lunch. Several varieties of commercial reduced-sodium soups are available if you don't have time to make your own. For spring or summer, you might prefer a fresh fruit or crisp green salad alongside the filled pita.

ZESTY GARDEN CHICKEN POCKETS

1½ cups cubed cooked chicken breast (about ¾ pound skinned, boned breasts)
½ cup coarsely shredded carrot
½ cup diced celery
2½ tablespoons plain low-fat yogurt
2 tablespoons commercial reduced-calorie Italian dressing
2 (6-inch) whole wheat pita bread rounds, cut in half crosswise

Combine first 3 ingredients in a bowl; toss. Combine yogurt and dressing; add to chicken mixture and toss. Cover and chill. Spoon ½ cup chicken mixture into each pita half. Yield: 4 servings.

PER SERVING: 155 CALORIES (16% FROM FAT)
FAT 2.8G (SATURATED FAT 0.8G)
PROTEIN 21.1G CARBOHYDRATE 9.2G
CHOLESTEROL 55MG SODIUM 232MG

Zesty Garden Chicken Pockets

Chicken Fajitas

CHICKEN FAJITAS

If chicken tenders are not available, buy 1 pound skinned, boned chicken breast halves, and cut the chicken into 3/4- to 1-inch strips.

4 (8-inch) flour tortillas
Vegetable cooking spray
1 pound chicken breast tenders
1 teaspoon chili powder
½ teaspoon ground cumin
½ teaspoon pepper
¼ teaspoon salt
1 tablespoon lime juice
⅔ cup sliced green onions
¼ cup chopped fresh cilantro
½ cup plain nonfat yogurt
4 leaf lettuce leaves
8 (⅛-inch-thick) slices unpeeled tomato,
     each cut in half crosswise

Wrap tortillas in damp paper towels and then in aluminum foil. Bake at 350° for 7 minutes or until softened; set aside.

Coat a large nonstick skillet with cooking spray; place over medium-high heat until hot. Add chicken, chili powder, and cumin; sauté 5 minutes or until chicken is done. Combine chicken, pepper, salt, and lime juice in a bowl, and toss well. Add green onions, cilantro, and yogurt, and toss well.

Place a lettuce leaf on each tortilla; divide chicken mixture evenly over lettuce. Top each with 4 tomato pieces; roll up. Yield: 4 servings.

PER SERVING: 290 CALORIES (15% FROM FAT)
FAT 4.8G (SATURATED FAT 0.9G)
PROTEIN 32.3G CARBOHYDRATE 28.3G
CHOLESTEROL 66MG SODIUM 446MG

FRENCH BREAD CHICKEN PIZZA

You can prepare this quick pizza in about 10 minutes plus 8 minutes cooking time. Ground turkey may be substituted for the ground thighs.

½ pound freshly ground raw chicken thighs
¼ cup chopped fresh cilantro
¼ teaspoon ground red pepper
1 (1-pound) loaf French bread (about 16
     inches long)
½ cup no-salt-added tomato sauce
2 tablespoons commercial pesto sauce
4 plum tomatoes, thinly sliced (about
     ½ pound)
½ cup (2 ounces) shredded part-skim
     mozzarella cheese
½ cup (2 ounces) shredded fontina or
     provolone cheese

Cook chicken in a medium-size nonstick skillet over medium heat until browned, stirring to crumble. Drain and pat dry with paper towels. Combine chicken, cilantro, and ground red pepper in a bowl; set aside.

Slice French bread in half lengthwise; place bread, cut side up, on a baking sheet. Broil 5½ inches from heat (with electric oven door partially opened) 1 minute or until lightly browned. Remove from oven, and set aside.

Combine tomato sauce and pesto sauce; stir well, and spread evenly over cut side of bread halves. Top with tomato slices and then the chicken mixture. Sprinkle with cheeses. Broil 5½ inches from heat 2 minutes or until cheese melts. Cut each bread half into 4 pieces. Yield: 8 servings.

PER SERVING: 287 CALORIES (27% FROM FAT)
FAT 8.6G (SATURATED FAT 3.4G)
PROTEIN 15.5G CARBOHYDRATE 35.1G
CHOLESTEROL 34MG SODIUM 482MG

CHICKEN AND EGGPLANT CALZONES

1 medium eggplant, peeled and cut into ½-inch
    slices (about 1 pound)
Vegetable cooking spray
1½ cups chopped cooked chicken breast
    (about 1 pound skinned, boned chicken
    breasts)
1 cup grated fresh Romano cheese
¼ cup chopped fresh basil
¼ cup chopped fresh parsley
⅛ teaspoon salt
¼ cup Chablis or other dry white wine
2 teaspoons olive oil
4 cloves garlic, minced
1 (1-pound) loaf commercial frozen white
    bread dough, thawed

    Arrange eggplant in a single layer on a baking
sheet coated with cooking spray. Coat surface of
eggplant with cooking spray. Bake at 425° for 17

minutes or until lightly browned. Dice eggplant,
and place in a large bowl. Add chicken and next 7
ingredients; stir well. Set aside.

    Divide dough into 8 equal portions. Working
with 1 portion at a time (cover remaining portions
to keep dough from drying out), roll each portion to
⅛-inch thickness. Place on a large baking sheet
coated with cooking spray, and pat into a 7-inch circle. Spoon ½ cup chicken mixture onto half of each
circle; moisten edges of dough with water. Fold
dough over filling; press edges together with a fork
to seal. Lightly coat with cooking spray.

    Bake at 375° for 18 minutes or until golden.
Remove from oven, and lightly coat again with
cooking spray. Serve warm. Yield: 8 servings.

PER SERVING: 307 CALORIES (27% FROM FAT)
FAT 9.3G (SATURATED FAT 3.6G)
PROTEIN 23.2G   CARBOHYDRATE 32.1G
CHOLESTEROL 51MG   SODIUM 524MG

Chicken and Eggplant Calzones

PROVENÇALE CHICKEN SANDWICHES

Team these sandwiches with a fresh fruit salad and iced tea for a refreshing summer luncheon.

1 (10½-ounce) can low-sodium chicken broth
½ pound skinned, boned chicken breast halves
1 tablespoon white wine vinegar
2 tablespoons finely chopped fresh parsley
1 teaspoon olive oil
⅛ teaspoon salt
¼ teaspoon dried whole thyme
⅛ teaspoon pepper
1 clove garlic, minced
4 curly leaf lettuce leaves
4 (1-ounce) slices Vienna bread
½ cup commercial roasted red bell peppers, thinly sliced into 2-inch strips
2 (⅛-inch-thick) slices purple onion, separated into rings

Bring chicken broth to a boil in a large saucepan over medium heat. Reduce heat, and add chicken; cover and simmer 10 to 15 minutes or until chicken is done. Remove chicken from saucepan; discard broth. Cut chicken crosswise into thin strips, and set aside.

Combine vinegar and next 6 ingredients in a large heavy-duty, zip-top plastic bag. Add chicken, and marinate in refrigerator at least 1 hour. Remove chicken from bag; set aside. Place 1 lettuce leaf on each of 2 slices of bread; top each with half of red bell pepper, half of the chicken, half of the onion rings, 1 lettuce leaf, and another slice of bread. Yield: 2 servings.

PER SERVING: 359 CALORIES (18% FROM FAT)
FAT 7.0G (SATURATED FAT 1.5G)
PROTEIN 34.1G   CARBOHYDRATE 37.8G
CHOLESTEROL 73MG   SODIUM 599MG

MARINATED CHICKEN SANDWICHES

It's easy to prepare a hurry-up lunch for two with this sandwich. The convenience comes from marinating boneless chicken in your favorite reduced-calorie salad dressing and then cooking it in the microwave.

2 (4-ounce) skinned, boned chicken breast halves (about 1 pound), skinned and boned
⅓ cup commercial reduced-calorie Italian dressing
Vegetable cooking spray
2 whole wheat hamburger buns, split
2 teaspoons reduced-calorie mayonnaise
2 teaspoons prepared mustard
Leaf lettuce

Place chicken in a shallow dish. Pour salad dressing over chicken; cover and marinate 6 to 8 hours in refrigerator.

Remove chicken from marinade. Place a browning grill or skillet in microwave oven; preheat at HIGH 4 to 5 minutes.

Coat grill with cooking spray; place chicken on grill. Microwave at HIGH 2 minutes. Turn chicken over, and give dish a half-turn; then microwave at HIGH 2½ to 3 minutes or until chicken is lightly browned and done.

Spread each bun half with ½ teaspoon mayonnaise and ½ teaspoon mustard. Place 1 lettuce leaf on each of 2 bun halves; top with chicken and remaining bun halves. Yield: 2 servings.

Note: Chicken may be broiled, if desired. Place on the rack of a broiler pan coated with cooking spray, and broil 5½ inches from heat (with electric oven door partially opened) 5 to 6 minutes on each side or until chicken is done.

PER SERVING: 327 CALORIES (26% FROM FAT)
FAT 9.4G (SATURATED FAT 2.3G)
PROTEIN 31.6G   CARBOHYDRATE 27.8G
CHOLESTEROL 91MG   SODIUM 1035MG

Chicken Club Sandwiches

CHICKEN CLUB SANDWICHES

2 tablespoons no-salt-added tomato juice
2 tablespoons balsamic vinegar
2 (4-ounce) skinned, boned chicken breast
   halves
Vegetable cooking spray
Dash of pepper
2 slices turkey bacon
6 (¾-ounce) slices light sourdough bread,
   toasted
1 tablespoon reduced-calorie mayonnaise
2 cups loosely packed torn romaine lettuce
8 (¼-inch-thick) slices tomato (about
   1 medium)

Combine tomato juice and vinegar in a shallow dish; set aside.

Place each piece of chicken between 2 sheets of heavy-duty plastic wrap, and flatten to ¼-inch thickness, using a meat mallet or rolling pin. Add chicken to vinegar mixture. Cover and marinate in refrigerator at least 1 hour, turning occasionally.

Remove chicken from marinade; discard marinade. Coat a large nonstick skillet with cooking spray, and place over medium heat until hot. Add chicken; cook 2 minutes on each side or until done. Remove from skillet, and sprinkle with pepper.

Cook turkey bacon until crisp according to package directions. Cut each bacon slice in half crosswise; set aside, and keep warm.

Spread 1 side of each of 2 slices of bread with ¾ teaspoon mayonnaise. Top each with ½ cup lettuce, 2 tomato slices, and 1 chicken breast half; cover with another slice of bread. Top each with ½ cup lettuce, 2 tomato slices, and 2 half-slices of bacon. Spread 1 side of remaining slices of bread with ¾ teaspoon mayonnaise; place on top of each sandwich. Cut each sandwich in half, and secure with wooden picks. Yield: 2 sandwiches.

PER SANDWICH: 353 CALORIES (30% FROM FAT)
FAT 11.9G (SATURATED FAT 2.3G)
PROTEIN 38.8G CARBOHYDRATE 22.9G
CHOLESTEROL 86MG SODIUM 918MG

BROILED CHICKEN SANDWICHES

1 (8-ounce) container plain nonfat yogurt
2 tablespoons lemon juice
1 tablespoon Dijon mustard
1 teaspoon dried whole tarragon
¼ teaspoon garlic powder
4 (4-ounce) skinned, boned chicken breast
   halves
8 canned medium-size mild Greek peppers
Vegetable cooking spray
4 green leaf lettuce leaves
4 reduced-calorie whole wheat hamburger
   buns, split
4 tomato slices (¼ inch thick)

Combine first 5 ingredients in a heavy-duty, zip-top plastic bag. Add chicken. Seal bag; marinate in refrigerator 8 hours, turning bag occasionally.

Remove stems from peppers; discard stems. Cut peppers into ¼-inch slices; set aside.

Remove chicken from marinade, discarding marinade. Place chicken on rack of a broiler pan coated with cooking spray. Broil chicken 5½ inches from heat (with electric oven door partially opened) 6 to 7 minutes on each side or until chicken is done.

Place lettuce leaves on bottom halves of hamburger buns. Place chicken breasts on lettuce, and top each with 1 tomato slice. Arrange pepper slices evenly over tomato. Top with remaining bun halves. Yield: 4 servings.

PER SERVING: 240 CALORIES (17% FROM FAT)
FAT 4.4G (SATURATED FAT 0.9G)
PROTEIN 29.6G CARBOHYDRATE 18.0G
CHOLESTEROL 73MG SODIUM 532MG

CURRIED CHICKEN SANDWICHES

Vegetable cooking spray
3 tablespoons finely chopped onion
2 teaspoons curry powder
¼ cup reduced-calorie mayonnaise
2 teaspoons chutney, chopped
¾ cup chopped cooked chicken breast
1 tablespoon chopped blanched almonds,
   toasted
8 slices whole wheat bread, trimmed

Coat a small nonstick skillet with cooking spray. Place over medium heat until hot. Add onion, and sauté 3 minutes or until tender. Add curry powder, and cook 1 minute, stirring constantly. Remove from heat; let cool.

Combine onion mixture, mayonnaise, and chutney in a bowl, stirring well. Add chicken and almonds, stirring well to combine. Spread 4 slices of bread evenly with chicken mixture; top with remaining bread slices. Cut each sandwich into 4 triangles or squares. Yield: 4 servings.

PER SERVING: 168 CALORIES (18% FROM FAT)
FAT 3.4G (SATURATED FAT 0.6G)
PROTEIN 16.4G CARBOHYDRATE 18.2G
CHOLESTEROL 36MG SODIUM 358MG

Sodium Alert

The sandwich's greatest enemy is often sodium, not fat. The basics of sandwich making—bread, lunchmeats, cheese, mustard, and mayonnaise—can pile on the sodium. Fat-free cheese and reduced-calorie condiments help slash fat and calories but not sodium. If you're watching your sodium intake, check the nutritional information for each recipe, and choose low-sodium accompaniments, such as carrot and celery sticks, rather than chips or pickles.

45

SUPER SALADS

*L*ooking for a rescue from another bowl of wilted lettuce and carrot sticks? For a light lunch, count on reliable chicken salad but not the old-fashioned variety. Reduced-calorie mayonnaise, low-fat yogurt, and vinaigrette dressing replace high-fat mayonnaise in these recipes. For a change of pace, try preparing chicken in various ways—grilled, blackened, or tossed with pasta. Our Chicken Caesar Salad (page 46), plus other recipes, will truly save you from tedious lunches or humdrum Sunday evening meals.

Grilled Chicken Piquant (Recipe follows on page 46)

GRILLED CHICKEN PIQUANT

(pictured on page 44)

4 (4-ounce) skinned, boned chicken breast
    halves
3 tablespoons lime juice
3 tablespoons lemon juice
1 tablespoon low-sodium soy sauce
1 tablespoon honey
2 teaspoons vegetable oil
¼ teaspoon ground ginger
¼ teaspoon ground cardamom
⅛ teaspoon ground coriander
1 cup shredded red cabbage
1 cup shredded Boston lettuce
1 cup shredded Bibb lettuce
1 cup shredded red leaf lettuce
1 small purple onion, thinly sliced
½ cup shredded carrot
Vegetable cooking spray

Place chicken in a shallow dish. Combine lime juice and next 7 ingredients in a small bowl, stirring well; pour over chicken. Cover and marinate in refrigerator 4 hours, turning occasionally.

Combine red cabbage, shredded lettuces, onion, and carrot; toss well. Cover and chill.

Drain chicken, reserving marinade. Coat grill rack with cooking spray, and place on grill over medium-hot coals. Place chicken on rack, and grill 5 to 6 minutes on each side or until chicken is tender. Set aside, and keep warm.

Place reserved marinade in a small saucepan. Bring marinade to a boil; reduce heat, and simmer 5 minutes. Spoon hot marinade over lettuce mixture, and toss gently.

Place lettuce mixture evenly on individual serving plates. Top lettuce mixture with grilled chicken breasts. Serve immediately. Yield: 4 servings.

PER SERVING: 204 CALORIES (25% FROM FAT)
FAT 5.6G (SATURATED FAT 1.3G)
PROTEIN 26.8G   CARBOHYDRATE 11.3G
CHOLESTEROL 70MG   SODIUM 168MG

CHICKEN CAESAR SALAD

4 (1-ounce) slices French bread
Vegetable cooking spray
½ teaspoon garlic powder
2 pounds skinned, boned chicken breasts
⅓ cup fresh lemon juice
¼ cup red wine vinegar
1 tablespoon olive oil
1 teaspoon anchovy paste
¼ teaspoon freshly ground pepper
5 cloves garlic
9 cups loosely packed torn romaine lettuce
¼ cup freshly grated Parmesan cheese

Trim bread crusts, and discard. Cut bread into 1-inch cubes. Arrange bread cubes in a single layer on a baking sheet. Coat bread cubes with cooking spray, and sprinkle with garlic powder; toss well. Bake at 350° for 15 minutes or until lightly browned; set aside.

Coat a large nonstick skillet with cooking spray; place over medium-high heat until hot. Add chicken; sauté 6 minutes on each side or until done. Remove chicken from skillet; let cool. Cut chicken across grain into thin slices; set aside.

Combine lemon juice and next 5 ingredients in container of an electric blender; cover and process until smooth. Add ¼ cup lemon juice mixture to chicken, tossing gently to coat.

Place lettuce in a large bowl; drizzle remaining lemon juice mixture over lettuce, and toss well. Add chicken mixture and cheese, tossing gently to coat. Serve with croutons. Yield: 7 servings.

PER SERVING: 257 CALORIES (28% FROM FAT)
FAT 7.9G (SATURATED FAT 2.1G)
PROTEIN 33.7G   CARBOHYDRATE 10.8G
CHOLESTEROL 85MG   SODIUM 303MG

BASIL CHICKEN SALAD

¼ cup plus 2 tablespoons nonfat mayonnaise
2 tablespoons fresh lemon juice
2 teaspoons Dijon mustard
¼ teaspoon hot sauce
⅛ teaspoon white pepper
3 cups chopped cooked chicken breast
½ cup chopped celery
¼ cup chopped green onions
¼ cup shredded fresh basil
6 cups shredded fresh spinach
1½ tablespoons pine nuts, toasted
Lemon wedges (optional)

Combine first 5 ingredients; stir well. Combine chicken, celery, green onions, and basil in a medium bowl. Add mayonnaise mixture; toss gently.

Place 1 cup spinach on 6 individual salad plates. Spoon chicken mixture over spinach. Sprinkle each serving with pine nuts. Garnish with lemon wedges, if desired. Yield: 6 servings.

PER SERVING: 159 CALORIES (23% FROM FAT)
FAT 4.1G (SATURATED FAT 1.0G)
PROTEIN 24.3G CARBOHYDRATE 5.6G
CHOLESTEROL 62MG SODIUM 329MG

Quick Tip

The cooktop and microwave oven are probably the easiest and quickest ways to cook chicken for a casserole, soup, sandwich, or salad. (See page 10 for basic instructions.) However, if you're really in a hurry, canned cooked chicken breast is available. But be aware that the sodium level is usually high in canned chicken.

TACO CHICKEN SALAD

6 (6-inch) corn tortillas
Vegetable cooking spray
½ teaspoon garlic powder
¼ teaspoon ground red pepper
½ cup chopped onion
4 cups shredded cooked chicken breast
2 (10-ounce) cans tomatoes and green chiles, drained and chopped
¾ cup nonfat sour cream alternative
6 cups torn iceberg lettuce
¼ cup plus 2 tablespoons (1½ ounces) shredded reduced-fat sharp Cheddar cheese
3 tablespoons minced fresh cilantro
¾ cup commercial mild no-salt-added salsa

Place tortillas on a large baking sheet. Bake at 350° for 6 minutes. Remove from oven; turn tortillas over, and coat lightly with cooking spray. Sprinkle garlic powder and red pepper evenly over tortillas. Bake an additional 6 minutes or until tortillas are crisp. Set aside.

Coat a large nonstick skillet with cooking spray; place over medium-high heat until hot. Add onion; sauté until tender. Add chicken and tomatoes and green chiles; stir well. Cook over medium heat until thoroughly heated, stirring frequently. Remove from heat; stir in sour cream.

Place tortillas on individual serving plates. Top each tortilla with 1 cup lettuce. Spoon chicken mixture evenly over lettuce. Sprinkle salads evenly with Cheddar cheese and cilantro. Serve salads with salsa. Yield: 6 servings.

PER SERVING: 258 CALORIES (18% FROM FAT)
FAT 5.3G (SAT. FAT 1.7G)
PROTEIN 31.0G CARBOHYDRATE 19.3G
CHOLESTEROL 71MG SODIUM 318MG

Chutney Chicken Salad

CHUTNEY CHICKEN SALAD

2 tablespoons chopped almonds
Vegetable cooking spray
1½ pounds skinned, boned chicken breasts
1 cup diagonally sliced celery
½ cup sliced green onions
1 (9-ounce) jar commercial mango chutney
6 cups loosely packed sliced romaine lettuce

Place chopped almonds on a baking sheet. Bake at 350° for 8 minutes or until toasted; set aside.

Coat a large nonstick skillet with cooking spray; place over medium heat until hot. Add chicken; cook 7 minutes on each side or until done. Remove chicken from skillet, and cut across grain into thin slices.

Combine almonds, chicken, celery, onions, and chutney in a large bowl; toss well to coat. Spoon chicken mixture onto individual lettuce-lined plates. Yield: 6 servings.

PER SERVING: 259 CALORIES (16% FROM FAT)
FAT 4.7G (SATURATED FAT 1.0G)
PROTEIN 28.6G CARBOHYDRATE 25.5G
CHOLESTEROL 72MG SODIUM 159MG

Menu Helper

From arugula to watercress, there are many salad greens from which to choose, and all are recommended for low-fat menus. Many of our recipes call for a particular salad green, but substitute others depending on your taste and on what's available.

CHICKEN AND ARUGULA SALAD

4 (4-ounce) skinned, boned chicken breast halves
1 tablespoon minced fresh thyme
1 tablespoon olive oil
3 tablespoons fresh lemon juice
1 tablespoon water
¼ teaspoon salt
⅛ teaspoon pepper
1 clove garlic, minced
Vegetable cooking spray
4 cups loosely packed arugula or leaf lettuce
½ cup vertically sliced purple onion
4 plum tomatoes, each cut into 8 wedges

Place chicken between 2 sheets of heavy-duty plastic wrap, and flatten to ¼-inch thickness, using a meat mallet or rolling pin. Place chicken in a shallow baking dish. Combine thyme and next 6 ingredients in a jar. Cover tightly, and shake vigorously. Drizzle 2 tablespoons thyme mixture over chicken; set aside remaining thyme mixture. Cover chicken, and marinate in refrigerator 1 hour.

Coat a nonstick skillet with cooking spray; place over medium heat until hot. Add chicken, and cook 3 minutes on each side or until done. Set aside, and keep warm.

Combine arugula, onion, tomato, and remaining 2 tablespoons thyme mixture in a bowl; toss well. Place 1½ cups arugula mixture on each of 4 serving plates. Cut each chicken breast half into ¼-inch slices; arrange on top of salad. Yield: 4 servings.

PER SERVING: 177 CALORIES (26% FROM FAT)
FAT 5.1G (SATURATED FAT 0.9G)
PROTEIN 27.2G CARBOHYDRATE 4.7G
CHOLESTEROL 66MG SODIUM 228MG

BLACKENED CHICKEN SALAD

1 teaspoon onion powder
½ teaspoon white pepper
½ teaspoon garlic powder
½ teaspoon dried whole oregano
½ teaspoon ground red pepper
½ teaspoon coarsely ground black pepper
4 (4-ounce) skinned, boned chicken breast
     halves
Vegetable cooking spray
¼ cup canned low-sodium chicken broth,
     undiluted
2 tablespoons balsamic vinegar
1 teaspoon cornstarch
2 teaspoons Dijon mustard
1 teaspoon olive oil
¼ teaspoon salt
8 cups loosely packed torn romaine lettuce
1 cup (2-inch) julienne-cut red bell pepper
¼ cup seeded, chopped unpeeled tomato

Combine first 6 ingredients; stir well. Rub chicken with spice mixture.

Coat a large cast-iron skillet with cooking spray; place over high heat until hot. Add chicken; cook 3 minutes on each side or until chicken is done. Remove chicken from skillet; let cool. Cut chicken across grain into thin slices; set aside.

Combine broth, vinegar, and cornstarch in a small saucepan. Bring to a boil over medium heat; cook 1 minute, stirring constantly. Remove from heat; stir in mustard, olive oil, and salt.

Combine chicken, vinegar mixture, lettuce, and bell pepper in a bowl; toss well to coat. Divide mixture evenly among 4 serving plates; top each with 1 tablespoon tomato. Yield: 4 servings.

PER SERVING: 199 CALORIES (26% FROM FAT)
FAT 5.8G (SATURATED FAT 1.3G)
PROTEIN 28.6G   CARBOHYDRATE 7.0G
CHOLESTEROL 72MG   SODIUM 302MG

Blackened Chicken Salad

CRISPY CHICKEN SALAD

½ cup fine, dry breadcrumbs
¼ teaspoon onion powder
¼ teaspoon garlic powder
¼ teaspoon dried whole thyme
1 egg white, lightly beaten
2 tablespoons skim milk
4 (4-ounce) skinned, boned chicken breast
    halves, cut into 1-inch strips
Vegetable cooking spray
2 cups shredded iceberg lettuce
2 cups shredded romaine lettuce
1 cup shredded red cabbage
¾ cup shredded carrot
¼ cup sliced green onions
⅓ cup white wine vinegar
1 tablespoon chopped fresh parsley
1 tablespoon olive oil
1 tablespoon Dijon mustard
1 teaspoon chopped fresh basil
¼ teaspoon freshly ground pepper

Combine first 4 ingredients in a shallow dish; stir well. Combine egg white and milk. Dip chicken in egg white mixture; dredge in breadcrumb mixture. Place chicken on a baking sheet coated with cooking spray. Bake at 350° for 35 minutes or until lightly browned.

Combine lettuces, cabbage, carrot, and green onions; toss well. Combine vinegar and remaining ingredients; pour over lettuce mixture, and toss well. Divide lettuce mixture evenly among individual serving plates. Top evenly with chicken strips. Yield: 4 servings.

PER SERVING: 246 CALORIES (22% FROM FAT)
FAT 6.1G (SATURATED FAT 1.0G)
PROTEIN 30.3G   CARBOHYDRATE 15.4G
CHOLESTEROL 67MG   SODIUM 312MG

TARRAGON CHICKEN SALAD

½ cup Chablis or other dry white wine
2 tablespoons minced shallots
1 tablespoon chopped fresh tarragon or
    1 teaspoon dried whole tarragon
¼ teaspoon salt
⅛ teaspoon pepper
4 cups chopped cooked chicken breast
1½ cups plain low-fat yogurt
½ small purple onion, cut into thin strips
2 cups water
¾ pound small round red potatoes, quartered
1 pound fresh green beans
1½ teaspoons vegetable oil
¼ teaspoon salt
⅛ teaspoon pepper

Combine first 5 ingredients in a small saucepan; cook over medium heat until liquid is absorbed, stirring constantly. Combine herb mixture, chicken, yogurt, and onion in a medium bowl; stir well. Cover and chill thoroughly.

Bring water to a boil in a medium saucepan. Add potato; cover, reduce heat, and simmer 10 minutes or until tender. Remove potato from liquid, reserving liquid. Set potato aside.

Wash beans; trim ends, and remove strings. Cut beans in half. Bring reserved liquid to a boil. Add beans; cover, reduce heat, and simmer 10 minutes or until crisp-tender. Drain.

Combine potato, beans, oil, ¼ teaspoon salt, and ⅛ teaspoon pepper in a large bowl; toss gently. Cover and chill thoroughly.

Spoon chicken mixture into center of a serving platter. Arrange bean mixture around chicken mixture. Yield: 8 servings.

PER SERVING: 193 CALORIES (18% FROM FAT)
FAT 3.9G (SATURATED FAT 1.3G)
PROTEIN 24.1G   CARBOHYDRATE 15.0G
CHOLESTEROL 57MG   SODIUM 231MG

Firecracker Chicken Salad

FIRECRACKER CHICKEN SALAD

This recipe can also be used as a tasty filling for sandwiches. Keep a tall, cool beverage nearby to balance the peppery bite.

4 (4-ounce) skinned, boned chicken breast
   halves
¼ teaspoon salt
¼ teaspoon cracked pepper
2 bay leaves
2 tablespoons plain nonfat yogurt
2 tablespoons reduced-calorie mayonnaise
2 tablespoons no-salt-added tomato sauce
1 tablespoon white wine vinegar
¼ teaspoon hot sauce
¼ teaspoon black pepper
⅛ teaspoon ground white pepper
1 large clove garlic, minced
⅓ cup thinly sliced celery
2 tablespoons sliced green onions
⅔ cup seeded, diced tomato
4 romaine lettuce leaves
Green onion fans (optional)

Place chicken in a medium saucepan; cover with water. Add salt, cracked pepper, and bay leaves. Bring to a boil; cover, reduce heat, and simmer 15 minutes or until chicken is done. Remove and discard bay leaves. Drain chicken, and set aside.

Combine yogurt and next 7 ingredients in a small bowl; stir well with a wire whisk. Set aside.

Tear chicken into bite-size pieces. Combine chicken, celery, and sliced green onions in a medium bowl; toss gently. Add yogurt mixture, stirring well. Cover and chill thoroughly. Stir in tomato just before serving. Serve on lettuce-lined salad plates. Garnish with green onion fans, if desired. Yield: 4 servings.

PER SERVING: 177 CALORIES (26% FROM FAT)
FAT 5.1G (SATURATED FAT 1.2G)
PROTEIN 27.0G CARBOHYDRATE 4.5G
CHOLESTEROL 73MG SODIUM 287MG

COUSCOUS AND CHICKEN SALAD

1½ cups water
1½ cups couscous, uncooked
2 cups shredded cooked dark meat chicken
   (about ¾ pound skinned, boned thighs)
2 cups shredded romaine lettuce
1 cup diced unpeeled tomato
⅔ cup finely chopped fresh parsley
⅓ cup chopped green onions
2 tablespoons finely chopped fresh mint
¼ cup plus 2 tablespoons lemon juice
3 tablespoons water
1½ tablespoons olive oil
½ teaspoon salt
¼ teaspoon pepper
1 small clove garlic, crushed

Bring water to a boil; stir in couscous. Remove from heat; let stand, covered, 5 minutes. Fluff with a fork.

Combine couscous and next 6 ingredients in a large bowl; toss gently. Combine lemon juice and next 5 ingredients in a jar; cover tightly, and shake vigorously. Pour over couscous mixture; toss well. Serve immediately. Yield: 6 (1⅓-cup) servings.

PER SERVING: 303 CALORIES (29% FROM FAT)
FAT 9.8G (SATURATED FAT 2.2G)
PROTEIN 20.5G CARBOHYDRATE 32.8G
CHOLESTEROL 54MG SODIUM 259MG

FYI

Couscous is rich in complex carbohydrates, low in fat, and very versatile. Try serving couscous as a side dish instead of rice or potatoes or as a cold salad with chopped vegetables, greens, and a commercial dressing. Couscous can even be cooked in milk, sweetened, and served with raisins as a hot breakfast cereal.

CHINESE CHICKEN-NOODLE SALAD

4 ounces angel hair pasta, uncooked
1 cup (½-inch) diagonally sliced fresh snow
    peas
2 cups shredded cooked chicken breast (about
    ¾ pound skinned, boned chicken breast)
½ cup diced sweet red pepper
¼ cup sliced green onions
1 medium cucumber, peeled, halved
    lengthwise, and sliced (about ¾ cup)
3 tablespoons low-sodium teriyaki sauce
2 tablespoons rice vinegar
2 teaspoons sesame seeds, toasted
1 teaspoon dark sesame oil
½ teaspoon salt
¼ teaspoon pepper

Break pasta into 5-inch pieces. Cook in boiling
water 2 minutes. Add snow peas; cook an additional
minute. Drain and rinse under cold running water;
drain well. Combine pasta mixture, chicken, and
next 3 ingredients in a bowl; set aside.

Combine teriyaki sauce and next 5 ingredients in
a bowl; stir well. Pour over pasta mixture, and toss
well. Serve at room temperature or chilled. Yield: 4
(1½-cup) servings.

PER SERVING: 273 CALORIES (16% FROM FAT)
FAT 4.8G (SATURATED FAT 1.0G)
PROTEIN 26.2G CARBOHYDRATE 29.5G
CHOLESTEROL 54MG SODIUM 640MG

BASIL CHICKEN-AND-PASTA SALAD

*Poaching the chicken in water, wine, and seasonings
keeps the chicken moist and imparts a wonderful
flavor and aroma. But you can bypass the poaching
by simply substituting 6 ounces of cooked chicken for
the first seven ingredients.*

¾ cup water
¼ cup Chablis or other dry white wine
¼ teaspoon dried whole basil
6 black peppercorns
1 bay leaf
1 clove garlic, halved
½ pound skinned, boned chicken breasts
2 tablespoons nonfat mayonnaise
2 tablespoons plain nonfat yogurt
1 tablespoon red wine vinegar
1 tablespoon olive oil
½ teaspoon spicy brown mustard
⅛ teaspoon salt
⅛ teaspoon pepper
1 cup cooked rotini (corkscrew pasta), cooked
    without salt or fat
1 cup cherry tomato halves
¼ cup thinly sliced green onions
Red leaf lettuce leaves

Combine first 6 ingredients in a large saucepan;
bring to a boil. Add chicken; cover, reduce heat,
and simmer 13 minutes or until chicken is done.
Remove chicken from saucepan; set aside. Strain
cooking liquid, reserving 2 tablespoons liquid.
Discard solids.

Chop chicken; set aside. Combine reserved cooking liquid, mayonnaise, and next 6 ingredients in a
large bowl; stir well. Add chicken, pasta, and next 2
ingredients; toss gently to coat. Serve at room temperature or chilled on lettuce-lined salad plates.
Yield: 2 servings.

PER SERVING: 330 CALORIES (25% FROM FAT)
FAT 9.1G (SATURATED FAT 1.4G)
PROTEIN 31.7G CARBOHYDRATE 29.7G
CHOLESTEROL 66MG SODIUM 452MG

Basil Chicken-and-Pasta Salad

Chicken-Pasta Salad

CHICKEN-PASTA SALAD

1½ cups farfalle (bow tie pasta), uncooked
¼ cup sun-dried tomato bits (without salt
   or oil)
½ cup hot water
1 teaspoon dried whole basil
¼ teaspoon salt
¼ teaspoon garlic powder
3 tablespoons white wine vinegar
2 teaspoons olive oil
⅛ teaspoon hot sauce
Vegetable cooking spray
1½ pounds unbreaded chicken breast nuggets
¾ cup coarsely chopped green pepper
1 tablespoon grated Parmesan cheese

Cook pasta according to package directions, omitting salt and fat; set aside.

Combine tomato bits and water in a bowl; cover and let stand 10 minutes. Drain. Add basil and next 5 ingredients; stir well, and set aside.

Coat a large nonstick skillet with cooking spray; place over medium-high heat until hot. Add chicken breast nuggets; sauté 5 minutes or until lightly browned. Add green pepper; sauté an additional 5 minutes or until chicken is done. Combine chicken mixture, pasta, and tomato mixture in a large bowl; toss gently.

Spoon 1 cup onto each of 6 serving plates; sprinkle each with ½ teaspoon cheese. Serve warm. Yield: 6 servings.

Note: Substitute 1½ pounds skinned, boned chicken breasts, cut into 1-inch pieces, for chicken nuggets, if desired.

Substitute 1 ounce finely diced whole sun-dried tomato (without salt or oil) for sun-dried tomato bits, if desired; omit salt.

PER SERVING: 232 CALORIES (17% FROM FAT)
FAT 4.5G (SATURATED FAT 0.9G)
PROTEIN 29.9G CARBOHYDRATE 16.8G
CHOLESTEROL 79MG SODIUM 298MG

CHICKEN SALAD IN ORANGE CUPS

2 medium oranges
1½ cups diced, cooked chicken breast
¼ cup chopped green pepper
¼ cup sliced green onions
3 tablespoons reduced-calorie mayonnaise
2 teaspoons unsweetened orange juice
2 teaspoons honey
½ teaspoon ground coriander
¼ teaspoon ground ginger
Fresh parsley sprigs (optional)

Cut oranges in half crosswise. Clip membranes, being careful not to puncture bottom. Remove pulp; set aside. Using kitchen shears, cut edges of orange cups into scallops. Set aside.

Dice reserved orange pulp. Combine pulp, chicken, pepper, and onions in a medium bowl. Combine mayonnaise, orange juice, honey, coriander, and ginger in a small bowl; stir well. Pour over chicken mixture; toss gently.

Divide chicken mixture evenly among orange cups. Cover and chill thoroughly. Garnish with parsley sprigs, if desired. Yield: 4 servings.

PER SERVING: 125 CALORIES (14% FROM FAT)
FAT 2.0G (SATURATED FAT 0.5G)
PROTEIN 16.8G CARBOHYDRATE 9.5G
CHOLESTEROL 45MG SODIUM 183MG

Quick Tip

While the orange cups above make for an innovative presentation, this salad is just as tasty (and easier to prepare) when served over lettuce leaves. You might also spoon chicken salad into cantaloupe halves or onto wedges of honeydew melon. For a different approach, try various combinations of this basic salad with other greens and fruit.

GRILLED CHICKEN AND SUMMER FRUIT

Grilled chicken and two kinds of melon make a perfect entrée for a summer supper. Substitute fresh strawberries for the raspberries, if preferred.

½ cup raspberry vinegar
¼ cup honey
2 tablespoons vegetable oil
1 teaspoon lemon juice
2 cups honeydew balls
2 cups cantaloupe balls
4 (4-ounce) skinned, boned chicken breast
    halves
Vegetable cooking spray
½ pound fresh spinach
½ cup fresh raspberries

Combine first 4 ingredients, and stir with a wire whisk; set aside.

Combine honeydew and cantaloupe balls. Pour ½ cup vinegar mixture over melon balls, tossing gently; reserve remaining vinegar mixture. Cover and chill.

Combine chicken breast halves and reserved vinegar mixture in a shallow dish; cover and marinate in refrigerator 30 minutes.

Coat grill rack with cooking spray; place on grill over medium-hot coals. Drain chicken, reserving marinade. Place chicken breast halves on rack, and grill 4 to 6 minutes on each side or until chicken is done, basting frequently with reserved marinade; set aside.

Arrange 1 chicken breast half and 1 cup drained melon mixture on each of 4 spinach-lined serving plates; top each with 2 tablespoons raspberries. Yield: 4 servings.

PER SERVING: 346 CALORIES (27% FROM FAT)
FAT 10.4G (SATURATED FAT 2.2G)
PROTEIN 28.3G CARBOHYDRATE 37.8G
CHOLESTEROL 70MG SODIUM 124MG

CHICKEN WALDORF SALAD

Keep the fiber high in this main dish salad by leaving the apple unpeeled.

¼ teaspoon unflavored gelatin
2 tablespoons cold water
3 tablespoons white wine vinegar
2½ tablespoons unsweetened apple juice
2 teaspoons vegetable oil
½ teaspoon sugar
¼ teaspoon salt
¼ teaspoon dry mustard
Dash of pepper
2 cups shredded cooked chicken breast (about
    1 pound skinned, boned chicken breasts)
1½ cups cubed unpeeled Red Delicious apple
½ cup sliced celery
½ cup halved seedless red grapes
3 tablespoons raisins
2 tablespoons chopped walnuts
4 cups loosely packed torn romaine lettuce

Sprinkle gelatin over 2 tablespoons cold water in a small saucepan; let stand 1 minute. Cook over low heat, stirring until gelatin dissolves. Combine gelatin mixture, vinegar, apple juice, and next 5 ingredients in a jar. Cover tightly; shake vigorously.

Combine chicken and next 5 ingredients in a large bowl; toss gently. Add gelatin mixture; toss gently. Arrange 1 cup lettuce on each of 4 salad plates; top each with an equal amount of chicken mixture. Yield: 4 servings.

PER SERVING 264 CALORIES (27% FROM FAT)
FAT 8.0G (SATURATED FAT 1.5G)
PROTEIN 28.9G CARBOHYDRATE 19.3G
CHOLESTEROL 72MG SODIUM 230MG

Chicken Waldorf Salad

Hot Chicken and Apple Salad

HOT CHICKEN AND APPLE SALAD

½ teaspoon paprika
¼ teaspoon pepper
⅛ teaspoon salt
1 pound skinned, boned chicken breasts, cut into bite-size pieces
3 tablespoons unsweetened apple cider
1 cup diagonally sliced carrots
3 cups cubed (½-inch-thick), unpeeled Granny Smith or other cooking apples (about 1 pound)
½ cup (2 ounces) crumbled Gorgonzola cheese, divided
2 tablespoons white wine vinegar
2 teaspoons minced shallots
4 cups torn fresh spinach

Combine paprika, pepper, and salt in a plastic bag; add chicken, and shake to coat. Set aside.

Place cider in an 8-inch square baking dish; microwave at HIGH 30 to 45 seconds. Add chicken; cover with wax paper, and microwave at MEDIUM-HIGH 6 to 7 minutes, stirring every 3 minutes. Drain chicken, and set aside, reserving apple cider mixture in baking dish.

Add carrot to cider mixture; cover with heavy-duty plastic wrap and vent. Microwave at HIGH 2 minutes. Stir in apple; microwave at HIGH 1½ to 2½ minutes or until apple is just tender. Drain, reserving 2 tablespoons apple cider mixture in baking dish.

Combine apple, carrot, chicken, and ¼ cup cheese in a bowl; toss and set aside. Add vinegar and shallots to reserved apple cider mixture in baking dish; microwave at HIGH 1 minute. Drizzle over chicken mixture; toss gently, and divide evenly among spinach-lined serving plates. Sprinkle each serving with 1 tablespoon cheese, and serve warm. Yield: 4 servings.

PER SERVING: 286 CALORIES (24% FROM FAT)
FAT 7.7G (SATURATED FAT 3.6G)
PROTEIN 30.9G   CARBOHYDRATE 24.3G
CHOLESTEROL 81MG   SODIUM 387MG

SPICY CARIBBEAN CHICKEN SALAD

French bread complements the distinct taste of this creamy salad.

2 cups water
4 green onions
1 pound skinned, boned chicken breasts
⅔ cup Chablis or other dry white wine
2 tablespoons minced jalapeño pepper
2 teaspoons sugar
½ teaspoon dried whole thyme
¼ teaspoon ground allspice
¼ teaspoon pepper
⅛ teaspoon ground cinnamon
⅛ teaspoon ground nutmeg
2 tablespoons cider vinegar
2 cloves garlic, minced
1 cup diced fresh pineapple
½ cup seedless red grapes, halved
½ cup nonfat mayonnaise
Romaine lettuce leaves (optional)
1 tablespoon sliced green onions

Combine 2 cups water and 4 green onions in a large skillet; bring to a boil over medium heat. Add chicken; cover, reduce heat, and simmer 15 minutes or until done. Remove chicken; set aside, and let cool. Discard the cooking liquid. Shred chicken into bite-size pieces, using 2 forks; set aside.

Combine wine and next 9 ingredients in a large heavy-duty, zip-top plastic bag. Add chicken; seal bag, and marinate in refrigerator 2 hours, turning bag occasionally. Drain; discard marinade.

Combine chicken, pineapple, grapes, and mayonnaise in a bowl; toss gently. Serve on a lettuce-lined plate, if desired. Top with sliced green onions. Yield: 4 servings.

PER SERVING: 218 CALORIES (17% FROM FAT)
FAT 4.1G (SATURATED FAT 1.1G)
PROTEIN 26.5G   CARBOHYDRATE 14.9G
CHOLESTEROL 72MG   SODIUM 448MG

SOUPS & STEWS

*E*ven today, homemade chicken soup remains a popular remedy for the common cold. You can't measure its medicinal value in a lab, but a steaming bowlful comforts with its aroma, soothes a sore throat, and warms the heart. These recipes for basic Chicken Noodle Soup (page 64) and other soups and stews, all delicious and healthy, are just what the doctor ordered.

For a complete meal, we "prescribe" combining soup with a low-fat sandwich or warm bread. You'll find other soups and stews, such as our Easy Chicken Chili (page 75) or Chicken Burgoo (page 76), hearty enough to serve as a one-dish meal with bread or a salad on the side. Chicken may not offer a miracle cure, but these combinations do work wonders at mealtime.

Chicken-Vegetable Soup (Recipe follows on page 67)

CHICKEN STOCK

3 quarts water
1 pound carrots, sliced
3 medium onions, peeled and quartered
1 (1-pound) bunch celery, cut into pieces
2 (3 to 3½ pound) broiler fryers
3 quarts water
1 large bunch fresh parsley
1 small bunch fresh dill

Combine first 4 ingredients in a 14-quart stock-pot. Bring to a boil; reduce heat to medium-low. Simmer, uncovered, 1 hour. Remove giblets from chickens; reserve for other uses. Rinse chickens well, and place in pot on top of vegetables (do not completely submerge chickens). Reduce heat to low; cover and cook 1 hour or until chickens are tender. Remove chickens; let cool.

Skin and bone chickens, reserving meat for other uses. Place chicken bones in pot. Add 3 quarts water; cover with parsley and dill. Cook, partially covered, over low heat 8 to 10 hours. Remove from heat and let cool.

Strain stock through a paper towel-lined sieve into a large bowl; discard bones and vegetables. Cover and chill stock. Skim solidified fat from top of stock, and discard. Yield: 1 gallon.

PER CUP: 22 CALORIES (0.0% FROM FAT)
FAT 0.0G (SATURATED FAT 0.0G)
PROTEIN 0.5G CARBOHYDRATE 1.9G
CHOLESTEROL 0MG SODIUM 5MG

FYI

When a recipe calls for canned no-salt-added or low-sodium chicken broth, you can substitute the homemade Chicken Stock above. The stock can be refrigerated for up to three days or frozen in convenient cup- or quart-size quantities. Defrost frozen stock in the refrigerator or microwave oven, and make sure you heat the stock to boiling before using it.

CHICKEN NOODLE SOUP

1 (3-pound) broiler-fryer, cut in half and skinned
1 large onion, cut into 8 wedges
6 sprigs fresh parsley
3 bay leaves
1 clove garlic, halved
8 whole black peppercorns
2 quarts water
Vegetable cooking spray
1 cup sliced carrot
¾ cup chopped celery
½ cup chopped onion
4 ounces medium egg noodles (uncooked)
½ cup frozen English peas, thawed
¾ teaspoon salt
½ teaspoon pepper
⅛ teaspoon rubbed sage

Combine first 7 ingredients in a Dutch oven. Bring mixture to a boil; cover, reduce heat, and simmer 45 to 50 minutes or until chicken is tender. Remove chicken from broth, reserving broth. Let chicken cool to touch. Bone chicken, and coarsely chop; set aside. Strain broth through a cheesecloth- or paper towel-lined sieve; discard onion and seasonings. Cover broth, and chill thoroughly. Skim and discard solidified fat from top of broth. Set broth aside.

Coat Dutch oven with cooking spray; place over medium-high heat until hot. Add carrot, celery, and onion; sauté until tender. Add chicken, reserved broth, noodles, peas, salt, pepper, and sage; bring to a boil. Reduce heat, and simmer, uncovered, 10 minutes or until noodles and peas are tender. Yield: 10 (1-cup) servings.

PER SERVING: 122 CALORIES (22% FROM FAT)
FAT 3.0G (SATURATED FAT 0.6G)
PROTEIN 11.9G CARBOHYDRATE 11.4G
CHOLESTEROL 40MG SODIUM 223MG

Place the first 7 ingredients in a Dutch oven to cook until the chicken is tender. As it simmers, this mixture will create a savory broth that will be the soup base.

Chill the strained broth mixture for several hours to allow the fat to condense on the surface. Defat the broth by skimming off the layer of fat that forms.

Sauté the vegetables until tender. This ensures the vegetables will be done; the soup does not cook much longer once the other ingredients are added.

Chicken Noodle Soup

SPRINGTIME CHICKEN SOUP

If fresh dillweed is not available, use ¹/₂ teaspoon dried whole dillweed instead.

4 (6-ounce) skinned chicken breast halves
1½ quarts water
1½ teaspoons chopped fresh dillweed
¾ teaspoon salt
¼ teaspoon pepper
¾ pound fresh asparagus, cut diagonally into 1-inch pieces
1 cup sliced green onions
3 medium tomatoes, peeled, seeded, and chopped
3 small yellow squash, cut into ½-inch slices
3 tablespoons lemon juice

Trim fat from chicken. Combine chicken, water, dillweed, salt, and pepper in a large Dutch oven. Bring to a boil. Cover; reduce heat, and simmer 30 minutes or until chicken is tender. Remove chicken from broth, and set broth aside. Bone chicken, and cut meat into bite-size pieces.

Combine chicken, reserved broth, asparagus, onions, tomato, and squash in a large Dutch oven. Bring to a boil. Cover, reduce heat, and simmer 20 minutes or until vegetables are tender. Stir in lemon juice. Yield: 12 (1-cup) servings.

PER SERVING: 72 CALORIES (10% FROM FAT)
FAT 0.8G (SATURATED FAT 0.2G)
PROTEIN 11.8G   CARBOHYDRATE 4.9G
CHOLESTEROL 26MG   SODIUM 182MG

CHICKEN MINESTRONE

3 ounces spaghetti (uncooked)
1 quart water
2 teaspoons chicken-flavored bouillon granules
½ teaspoon dried whole basil
½ teaspoon dried whole oregano
1 (10-ounce) package frozen mixed vegetables
1 pound fresh mushrooms, sliced
2 cups cubed cooked chicken breast
2 medium zucchini, sliced
1 (16-ounce) can tomatoes, undrained and chopped

Break spaghetti into pieces; combine spaghetti and next 5 ingredients in a Dutch oven. Bring to a boil. Cover; reduce heat, and simmer 5 minutes. Add mushrooms, chicken, zucchini, and tomato. Cover, reduce heat, and simmer 5 minutes or until tender. Yield: 9 (1-cup) servings.

PER SERVING: 163 CALORIES (16% FROM FAT)
FAT 2.9G (SATURATED FAT 0.7G)
PROTEIN 17.8G   CARBOHYDRATE 16.7G
CHOLESTEROL 37MG   SODIUM 300MG

Microwave Magic

To prepare cooked chicken to use as an ingredient in a recipe, determine how much chicken you need. Count on ½ cup chopped chicken per chicken breast half. Chicken cooks quickly with the help of a microwave oven. To microwave chicken for the above recipe, arrange four boned and skinned chicken breast halves in a baking dish. Microwave, covered, at HIGH 6 to 7 minutes or until done, turning dish once. (See page 10 for other basic cooking instructions.)

CHICKEN POSOLE

3 (6-ounce) skinned chicken breast halves
1 medium onion, sliced
3 cloves garlic, minced
1 teaspoon chicken-flavored bouillon granules
¼ teaspoon pepper
4 cups water
1 (16-ounce) can white hominy, drained
½ cup chopped sweet red pepper
½ cup chopped sweet yellow pepper
1 tablespoon chili powder
1 teaspoon ground cumin
1 teaspoon dried whole oregano
1 teaspoon dried whole coriander
¼ teaspoon salt
1¾ cups seeded, chopped tomato
1½ cups finely shredded iceberg lettuce
¼ cup plus 2 tablespoons sliced radish

Combine first 6 ingredients in a Dutch oven. Bring to a boil; cover, reduce heat, and simmer 35 minutes or until chicken is tender. Remove chicken from broth; skim fat from broth, reserving broth. Bone chicken, and chop.

Combine reserved broth, chicken, hominy, sweet red pepper, sweet yellow pepper, chili powder, ground cumin, oregano, coriander, and salt in pan, stirring well. Bring to a boil; cover, reduce heat, and simmer 20 minutes. Stir in chopped tomato; cook, uncovered, 5 minutes. Ladle soup into individual bowls. Top each serving with ¼ cup chopped lettuce and 1 tablespoon sliced radish. Yield: 6 (1-cup) servings.

PER SERVING: 171 CALORIES (17% FROM FAT)
FAT 3.2G (SATURATED FAT 0.7G)
PROTEIN 18.0G CARBOHYDRATE 17.7G
CHOLESTEROL 42MG SODIUM 434MG

CHICKEN-VEGETABLE SOUP

(pictured on page 62)

This soup can be made ahead and frozen. Freeze the soup in quart containers. Defrost when needed, and reheat to serve.

3½ cups water
1 tablespoon chicken-flavored bouillon granules
1 (14½-ounce) can no-salt-added whole tomatoes, undrained and chopped
¼ cup instant minced onion
1 teaspoon dried whole basil
1 teaspoon paprika
¾ teaspoon instant minced garlic
¼ teaspoon salt
1 cup sliced carrots
1 (8-ounce) can mushroom stems and pieces, drained
1 cup diced zucchini
1 cup diced, cooked chicken
2 tablespoons Burgundy or other dry red wine

Combine water, bouillon granules, tomato, onion, basil, paprika, garlic, and salt in a Dutch oven. Bring to a boil; cover, reduce heat, and simmer 10 minutes. Add carrot; cover and simmer 10 minutes. Add mushrooms, zucchini, chicken, and wine; simmer, uncovered, 8 minutes. Yield: 7 (1-cup) servings.

PER SERVING: 82 CALORIES (23% FROM FAT)
FAT 2.1G (SATURATED FAT 0.5G)
PROTEIN 7.3G CARBOHYDRATE 9.8G
CHOLESTEROL 16MG SODIUM 471MG

Mexican Chicken Soup

MEXICAN CHICKEN SOUP

1 teaspoon ground cumin
1 teaspoon chili powder
2 teaspoons cider vinegar
½ teaspoon ground cinnamon
2 teaspoons vegetable oil
2¼ pounds chicken thighs, skinned, boned,
      and cut into bite-size pieces
2½ cups slivered onion (about 1 large)
4 cloves garlic, minced
6½ cups canned no-salt-added chicken broth
4 cups chopped zucchini
1½ cups frozen whole kernel corn, thawed
1 tablespoon minced pickled jalapeño peppers
¾ teaspoon salt
¼ teaspoon dried whole oregano
1 (14½-ounce) can no-salt-added whole
      tomatoes, undrained and chopped
½ cup plus 2 tablespoons (2½ ounces)
      shredded reduced-fat Monterey Jack
      cheese

Combine cumin, chili powder, cider vinegar, and cinnamon in a small bowl; stir well.

Heat oil in a large Dutch oven over medium-high heat. Add chicken, onion, garlic, and cumin mixture; sauté 5 minutes. Add broth and next 6 ingredients; bring to a boil. Reduce heat, and simmer, uncovered, 20 minutes, stirring occasionally.

Ladle soup into bowls; top each serving with 1 tablespoon cheese. Yield: 10 (1½-cup) servings.

Note: To save time, you may purchase 1¼ pounds chicken thighs that are already skinned and boned.

PER SERVING: 167 CALORIES (27% FROM FAT)
FAT 5.1G (SATURATED FAT 1.6G)
PROTEIN 16.4G CARBOHYDRATE 13.1G
CHOLESTEROL 52MG SODIUM 310MG

SACRAMENTO TACO SOUP

Serve a tossed green salad with this hearty soup for a satisfying lunch or light dinner.

1 pound skinned, boned chicken breasts, cut into bite-size pieces
2 (14½-ounce) cans no-salt-added whole tomatoes, undrained and chopped
2 (13¾-ounce) cans no-salt-added chicken broth
1 (4-ounce) can chopped green chiles, undrained
¼ teaspoon salt
4 (6-inch) corn tortillas, halved
½ cup chopped green onions
½ cup (2 ounces) shredded reduced-fat Monterey Jack cheese
¼ cup chopped fresh cilantro
¼ cup commercial green taco sauce

Combine first 5 ingredients in a large saucepan; stir well. Bring to a boil; reduce heat, and simmer, uncovered, 30 minutes.

For each serving, cut 1 tortilla half into 1-inch pieces, and place in a soup bowl. Add 1 cup soup; top with 1 tablespoon green onions, 1 tablespoon cheese, 1½ teaspoons cilantro, and 1½ teaspoons green taco sauce. Yield: 8 (1-cup) servings.

PER SERVING: 157 CALORIES (14% FROM FAT)
FAT 2.4G (SATURATED FAT 1.0G)
PROTEIN 17.2G   CARBOHYDRATE 15.5G
CHOLESTEROL 38MG   SODIUM 291MG

Sacramento Taco Soup

Chunky Chicken-Potato Soup

CHUNKY CHICKEN-POTATO SOUP

3 medium baking potatoes, peeled and cubed
2 cups chopped onion
4 cups water
1 tablespoon chicken-flavored bouillon
    granules
¼ teaspoon salt
¼ teaspoon ground red pepper
⅛ teaspoon pepper
2 cups chopped cooked chicken breast
¼ cup skim milk
2 tablespoons plus 2 teaspoons chopped
    pimiento
⅓ cup low-fat sour cream
⅓ cup (1⅓ ounces) shredded 40% less-fat
    Cheddar cheese
2 tablespoons plus 2 teaspoons chopped fresh
    chives

Combine first 7 ingredients in a large Dutch oven; bring to a boil. Cover; reduce heat, and simmer 30 minutes or until potato is tender.

Place half of potato mixture in container of an electric blender or food processor; cover and process until smooth. Add pureed mixture, chicken, and milk to remaining potato mixture in Dutch oven; cook over medium heat until thoroughly heated. Stir in pimiento.

Ladle soup into serving bowls. Top each serving with 2 teaspoons sour cream, 2 teaspoons cheese, and 1 teaspoon chives. Yield: 8 (1-cup) servings.

PER SERVING: 177 CALORIES (20% FROM FAT)
FAT 4.0G (SATURATED FAT 1.7G)
PROTEIN 16.9G CARBOHYDRATE 19.0G
CHOLESTEROL 43MG SODIUM 459MG

CHEESY CHICKEN AND RICE CHOWDER

This recipe uses pureed vegetables and low-fat milk to provide a thick, rich consistency without the addition of high-fat cream.

Vegetable cooking spray
1 pound skinned, boned chicken breast, cubed
1 cup sliced green onions
1 cup chopped onion
1 clove garlic, minced
2 cups peeled, chopped turnip (about 1 pound)
1 cup peeled, chopped round red potato (about
    6 ounces)
½ cup long-grain rice, uncooked
3 (10½-ounce) cans low-sodium chicken broth
1 cup 2% low-fat milk
¾ cup (3 ounces) shredded extra-sharp
    Cheddar cheese
¼ cup all-purpose flour
½ teaspoon salt
¼ teaspoon pepper
2 teaspoons dry sherry

Coat a large Dutch oven with cooking spray; place over medium-high heat until hot. Add chicken and next 3 ingredients; sauté 8 minutes or until onion is tender and chicken loses its pink color. Remove from pan; set aside. Add turnip and next 3 ingredients to pan; bring to a boil. Cover, reduce heat, and simmer 20 minutes or until vegetables are tender.

Place 3 cups turnip mixture in container of an electric blender; cover and process until smooth. Add turnip puree back to mixture in pan; stir well. Add chicken mixture, milk, and next 4 ingredients; stir well. Cook over medium heat, stirring constantly, 5 minutes or until mixture is hot and cheese melts. Stir in sherry. Yield: 6 (1½-cup) servings.

PER SERVING: 307 CALORIES (23% FROM FAT)
FAT 7.8G (SATURATED FAT 4.1G)
PROTEIN 27.0G CARBOHYDRATE 31.1G
CHOLESTEROL 62MG SODIUM 438MG

SAVORY CHICKEN STEW

1 (3½-pound) broiler-fryer, skinned
2 quarts plus 1 cup water, divided
3 medium carrots, scraped and cut into
   1-inch pieces
2 medium onions, quartered
2 stalks celery, cut into 1-inch pieces
¾ teaspoon dried whole tarragon
¼ teaspoon salt
⅛ teaspoon pepper
⅓ cup skim milk
3 tablespoons all-purpose flour

Remove giblets and neck from chicken, and reserve for other uses. Trim excess fat from chicken. Place chicken in a large Dutch oven. Add 2 quarts water. Bring to a boil. Cover; reduce heat, and simmer 45 minutes or until chicken is tender.

Remove chicken from Dutch oven, and let cool to touch. Reserve 3 cups stock in Dutch oven. Skim fat from top of stock and discard.

Bone and cut chicken into 1-inch pieces. Add chicken pieces, 1 cup water, carrot, onion, celery, tarragon, salt, and pepper to stock in Dutch oven. Bring to a boil. Cover; reduce heat, and simmer stew 1 hour.

Combine skim milk and flour, stirring until well blended. Add to stew. Cook over medium-high heat, stirring constantly, until thickened and bubbly. Yield: 6 (1-cup) servings.

PER SERVING: 234 CALORIES (28% FROM FAT)
FAT 7.2G (SATURATED FAT 2.0G)
PROTEIN 29.2G   CARBOHYDRATE 11.9G
CHOLESTEROL 84MG   SODIUM 212MG

EASY BRUNSWICK STEW

4 (6-ounce) skinned chicken breast halves
4 cups water
1 cup chopped onion
¾ cup diced green pepper
2 teaspoons chicken-flavored bouillon granules
1 teaspoon pepper
1 (14½-ounce) can no-salt-added whole
   tomatoes, undrained and chopped
1½ cups frozen whole kernel corn
1 cup frozen baby lima beans
2 tablespoons vinegar
¼ teaspoon ground red pepper
2 tablespoons all-purpose flour
2 tablespoons water

Trim excess fat from chicken. Combine chicken and next 5 ingredients in a large Dutch oven. Bring to a boil; cover, reduce heat, and simmer 25 minutes or until chicken is tender. Remove chicken from broth; skim fat from broth, and set broth aside. Bone chicken, and cut into bite-size pieces.

Combine chicken, broth, tomato, corn, lima beans, vinegar, and red pepper in pan. Bring to a boil; cover, reduce heat, and simmer 15 minutes.

Combine flour and 2 tablespoons water, stirring until smooth. Add to stew, and stir well. Cook over medium heat until thickened and bubbly, stirring constantly. Yield: 9 (1-cup) servings.

PER SERVING: 144 CALORIES (14% FROM FAT)
FAT 2.2G (SATURATED FAT 0.6G)
PROTEIN 17.0G   CARBOHYDRATE 14.7G
CHOLESTEROL 38MG   SODIUM 249MG

Lighten Up

Reduce fat in soups and stews by using a gravy strainer, a fat-separating cup, or a fat-off ladle. Another way to remove excess fat from the soup pot is to chill the mixture overnight in the refrigerator. The fat will rise to the top and harden during chilling; skim or lift it off with a spoon.

Rustic Chicken and Macaroni Stew

1 pound skinned, boned chicken breasts
½ teaspoon cracked pepper
Olive oil-flavored vegetable cooking spray
1 teaspoon olive oil
1½ cups chopped onion
1 clove garlic, minced
2 cups coarsely chopped carrot
2 cups coarsely chopped celery
¼ cup chopped fresh parsley
½ teaspoon dried whole thyme
1 bay leaf
3 cups canned low-sodium chicken broth, undiluted
½ cup Chablis or other dry white wine
1 tablespoon balsamic vinegar
½ cup elbow macaroni, uncooked
¼ cup sliced ripe olives
2 tablespoons plus 1 teaspoon freshly grated Parmesan cheese

Cut chicken into 1-inch pieces, and sprinkle with pepper. Coat a large Dutch oven with cooking spray; add olive oil. Place over medium heat until hot. Add chicken, and cook until chicken is browned on all sides, stirring frequently. Drain and pat dry with paper towels. Wipe drippings from pan with a paper towel.

Coat pan with cooking spray; place over medium-high heat until hot. Add onion and garlic; sauté until tender.

Add chicken, carrot, and next 7 ingredients, stirring well. Bring to a boil; cover, reduce heat, and simmer 25 minutes or until vegetables are tender. Add macaroni and olives; cover and cook an additional 10 minutes or until macaroni is tender. Remove and discard bay leaf. Ladle stew into individual bowls. Sprinkle each serving with 1 teaspoon cheese. Yield: 7 (1-cup) servings.

Per Serving: 174 Calories (20% from fat)
Fat 3.8g (Saturated Fat 1.1g)
Protein 18.0g Carbohydrate 16.9g
Cholesterol 37mg Sodium 193mg

Picadillo Chicken Stew

1 pound skinned, boned chicken breasts, cut into 1-inch pieces
1 teaspoon ground cumin
1 teaspoon ground coriander
1 teaspoon chili powder
¼ teaspoon salt
⅛ teaspoon ground cinnamon
Vegetable cooking spray
2 teaspoons olive oil
1 cup coarsely chopped onion
2 cloves garlic, minced
1 (14½-ounce) can no-salt-added whole tomatoes, undrained and chopped
½ cup golden raisins
½ cup canned low-sodium chicken broth, undiluted
2 tablespoons finely chopped canned jalapeño pepper
2 tablespoons sliced almonds, toasted

Combine first 6 ingredients in a bowl; toss well, and set aside. Coat a nonstick skillet with cooking spray; add olive oil, and place over medium-high heat until hot. Add chicken mixture; sauté 2 minutes. Add onion and garlic; sauté 2 minutes. Add tomato and next 3 ingredients; stir well. Reduce heat, and cook, uncovered, 15 minutes or until thickened, stirring occasionally.

Ladle soup into bowls; top each serving with 1½ teaspoons almonds. Serve with toasted corn tortilla wedges, if desired. Yield: 4 (1-cup) servings.

Per Serving: 274 Calories (20% from fat)
Fat 6.0g (Saturated Fat 0.9g)
Protein 29.4g Carbohydrate 27.2g
Cholesterol 66mg Sodium 263mg

Chunky Chicken Chili

CHUNKY CHICKEN CHILI

Vegetable cooking spray
1½ cups chopped onion
1 cup chopped green pepper
3 jalapeño peppers, chopped
3 cloves garlic, minced
2 tablespoons chili powder
2 teaspoons ground cumin
½ teaspoon dried whole oregano
2 cups bite-size cooked chicken breast (about
    1 pound skinned, boned chicken breasts)
2 cups bite-size cooked chicken thigh (about 1
    pound skinned, boned chicken thighs)
1 cup water
¼ to ½ teaspoon ground red pepper
¼ teaspoon black pepper
1 tablespoon Worcestershire sauce
1 tablespoon Dijon mustard
1 (14½-ounce) can no-salt-added stewed
    tomatoes
1 (13¾-ounce) can no-salt-added chicken
    broth
1 (12-ounce) bottle reduced-calorie chili sauce
1 (16-ounce) can Great Northern beans,
    drained
1¼ cups peeled, diced avocado
1¼ cups chopped purple onion
½ cup plus 1 tablespoon plain nonfat yogurt

Coat a Dutch oven with cooking spray; place over medium heat until hot. Add onion and next 3 ingredients; sauté 5 minutes. Add chili powder, cumin, and oregano; cook 2 minutes. Add chicken, 1 cup water, and next 7 ingredients; bring to a boil. Cover, reduce heat, and simmer 20 minutes.

Add beans, and cook 5 minutes. Ladle chili into individual soup bowls; top each with about 2 table-spoons avocado, 2 tablespoons onion, and 1 table-spoon yogurt. Yield: 9 (1-cup) servings.

PER SERVING: 300 CALORIES (29% FROM FAT)
FAT 9.8G (SATURATED FAT 2.2G)
PROTEIN 27.4G CARBOHYDRATE 26.2G
CHOLESTEROL 68MG SODIUM 289MG

EASY CHICKEN CHILI

Vegetable cooking spray
1 cup chopped green pepper
¾ cup chopped celery
½ cup chopped carrot
½ cup chopped onion
1 pound ground raw chicken
2 teaspoons chili powder
1 teaspoon dried Italian seasoning
1¼ cups vegetable cocktail juice
1 (8-ounce) can no-salt-added tomato sauce

Coat a large nonstick skillet with cooking spray; place over medium-high heat until hot. Add next 4 ingredients; sauté 8 minutes or until tender. Add chicken and next 2 ingredients; cook 2 minutes or until chicken is browned, stirring to crumble. Add remaining ingredients; reduce heat, and simmer, uncovered, 30 minutes or until thickened, stirring occasionally. Yield: 4 (1-cup) servings.

PER SERVING: 116 CALORIES (19% FROM FAT)
FAT 2.4G (SATURATED FAT 1.0G)
PROTEIN 15.0G CARBOHYDRATE 8.6G
CHOLESTEROL 45MG SODIUM 237MG

Quick Tip

Many soups, stews, chilies, and gumbos are excellent make-ahead dishes because they taste even better after being refrigerated overnight. If you're entertaining or juggling a hectic schedule, make soups in advance to simplify meal preparation.

CHICKEN BURGOO

¼ pound lean round steak (½-inch thick)
¼ pound veal cutlets, cut into 1-inch cubes
¼ pound lean boneless pork shoulder, cut into
   1-inch cubes
4 (6-ounce) skinned chicken breast halves
1½ quarts water
1 (14½-ounce) can no-salt-added whole
   tomatoes, undrained
1 (8¾-ounce) can whole kernel corn, drained
1 small onion, chopped
1 medium carrot, scraped and thinly sliced
¾ cup thinly sliced fresh okra
¾ cup shredded cabbage
½ cup peeled, cubed red potato
½ cup frozen lima beans, thawed
½ cup chopped green pepper
¼ cup chopped fresh parsley
2 hot red pepper pods
2½ teaspoons low-sodium Worcestershire
   sauce
¼ teaspoon salt
⅛ teaspoon ground red pepper

Trim fat from steak. Cut steak into 1-inch pieces. Combine steak with veal, pork, chicken, and water in a Dutch oven; bring mixture to a boil. Cover; reduce heat, and simmer 30 minutes or until tender. Remove meat and chicken; skim fat from broth. Reserve broth. Bone chicken; cut into bite-size pieces.

Combine meat, chicken, reserved broth, tomato, and remaining ingredients in a large Dutch oven. Bring to a boil. Uncover, reduce heat, and simmer 2½ hours or until thickened, stirring occasionally. Discard pepper pods. Yield: 10 (1-cup) servings.

PER SERVING: 192 CALORIES (13% FROM FAT)
FAT 2.7G (SATURATED FAT 0.8G)
PROTEIN 22.5G CARBOHYDRATE 19.1G
CHOLESTEROL 55MG SODIUM 206MG

CHICKEN AND DUMPLINGS

6½ cups water, divided
4 (8-ounce) chicken breast halves
1½ cups sliced fresh mushrooms
¾ cup diced carrot
2 tablespoons chopped onion
¾ teaspoon poultry seasoning
½ teaspoon salt
½ teaspoon pepper
1 teaspoon lemon juice
4 drops of hot sauce
1 clove garlic, minced
1¼ cups plus 2 tablespoons all-purpose flour,
   divided
1 teaspoon baking powder
½ cup skim milk

Place 6 cups water and next 4 ingredients in a large Dutch oven. Bring to a boil; cover, reduce heat, and simmer 45 minutes or until chicken is tender. Remove chicken breast halves from broth, and let each cool separately. Discard skin and bones; cut chicken into bite-size pieces, and add to vegetable mixture. Cover and chill 8 hours.

Skim fat from broth and discard. Stir in poultry seasoning and next 5 ingredients.

Combine ¼ cup plus 2 tablespoons flour and remaining ½ cup water; stir well. Bring chicken mixture to a boil; stir in flour mixture. Reduce heat, and simmer chicken mixture, uncovered, 35 minutes or until thickened.

Combine remaining 1 cup flour and baking powder; add milk, stirring just until dry ingredients are moistened. Drop batter by teaspoonfuls into boiling broth; cover, reduce heat, and simmer 15 minutes or until dumplings are tender. Yield: 6 (1½-cup) servings.

PER SERVING: 258 CALORIES (12% FROM FAT)
FAT 3.3G (SATURATED FAT 1.0G)
PROTEIN 29.2G CARBOHYDRATE 26.0G
CHOLESTEROL 69MG SODIUM 273MG

Chicken and Dumplings

OVEN FAVORITES

"Reliable." "Tried and true." "Predictable." "Stand-by." "Can't miss." "No fail." "Fool proof." A host of clichés label the all-too-familiar roasted whole chicken and basic chicken casserole.

If you long to escape the mundane, look no further. With all of the flavor and little of the fat, these recipes command attention whether you fancy Chicken-Vegetable Strudel (page 98), Light Enchiladas (page 98), or Chicken en Papillote (page 92). This chapter also introduces new ideas for casseroles and easy baked chicken. Who said oven entrées had to be boring?

Chicken Linguine (Recipe follows on page 93)

GLAZED ROASTED CHICKEN
(pictured on page 2)

1 (3-pound) broiler-fryer, skinned
1 large carrot, scraped and cut into 3 pieces
1 large stalk celery, cut into 3 pieces
1 small onion, quartered
2 cloves garlic, halved
Vegetable cooking spray
¼ cup low-sugar apple spread
1 tablespoon white wine Worcestershire sauce
1 teaspoon margarine
Fresh sage sprigs (optional)
Fresh thyme sprigs (optional)

Remove giblets and neck from chicken; reserve for other uses. Rinse chicken under cold water; pat dry with paper towels.

Lightly stuff chicken with carrot, celery, onion, and garlic. Close with skewers; tie ends of legs together with string. Lift wingtips up and over back of chicken, tucking wingtips under chicken.

Carefully transfer chicken, breast side up, to a rack in a shallow roasting pan coated with cooking spray; insert a meat thermometer into meaty part of thigh, making sure it does not touch bone.

Combine apple spread, Worcestershire sauce, and margarine in a saucepan. Cook over low heat until apple spread melts. Set aside half of mixture; brush chicken with remaining mixture.

Cover chicken with aluminum foil, and bake at 375° for 45 minutes; uncover and bake an additional 45 minutes or until meat thermometer registers 185°, basting with reserved mixture. Remove skewers and string; discard vegetables. Transfer chicken to a serving platter; garnish with sage and thyme, if desired. Yield: 6 servings.

PER SERVING: 243 CALORIES (34% FROM FAT)
FAT 9.1G (SATURATED FAT 2.4G)
PROTEIN 32.9G CARBOHYDRATE 5.4G
CHOLESTEROL 101MG SODIUM 140MG

GREEK-SEASONED CHICKEN WITH ORZO

Vegetable cooking spray
1 (3-pound) broiler-fryer, cut up and skinned
2 tablespoons lemon juice
2 tablespoons reduced-calorie margarine, melted
1 teaspoon commercial Greek-style seasoning
¾ teaspoon paprika
1 cup orzo (uncooked)
¼ cup sliced pitted ripe black olives
1½ tablespoons chopped fresh chives
1 tablespoon reduced-calorie margarine
¾ teaspoon commercial Greek-style seasoning

Coat a 13- x 9- x 2-inch baking dish with cooking spray. Place chicken pieces in dish. Combine lemon juice, 2 tablespoons margarine, 1 teaspoon Greek-style seasoning, and paprika; stir well. Pour mixture evenly over chicken pieces.

Cover and bake at 350° for 30 minutes. Uncover and bake an additional 35 minutes or until chicken is done, basting frequently with pan juices.

Cook orzo according to package directions, omitting salt and fat; drain. Combine orzo, olives, chives, 1 tablespoon margarine, and ¾ teaspoon Greek-style seasoning; toss gently.

Serve chicken over orzo. Spoon any remaining pan juices over chicken. Yield: 6 servings.

PER SERVING: 300 CALORIES (25% FROM FAT)
FAT 8.2G (SATURATED FAT 1.5G)
PROTEIN 27.9G CARBOHYDRATE 27.4G
CHOLESTEROL 76MG SODIUM 866MG

Greek-Seasoned Chicken with Orzo

TEX-MEX ROASTED CHICKEN WITH VEGETABLES

1 (3-pound) broiler-fryer, skinned
Vegetable cooking spray
1 tablespoon white wine vinegar
1 teaspoon ground cumin
1 teaspoon chili powder
½ teaspoon dried whole basil
½ teaspoon dried whole oregano
¼ teaspoon salt
Vegetable cooking spray
2 cups coarsely chopped yellow squash
2 cups coarsely chopped zucchini
1½ cups unpeeled, seeded, coarsely chopped tomato
1 small sweet red pepper, cut into julienne strips
½ cup chopped shallots

Trim fat from chicken. Remove giblets and neck from chicken; reserve for other uses. Rinse chicken under cold water; pat dry. Place chicken, breast side up, on a rack in a roasting pan coated with cooking spray. Truss chicken. Insert meat thermometer in meaty part of thigh, making sure it does not touch bone.

Combine vinegar and next 5 ingredients; rub chicken with herb mixture. Bake, uncovered, at 375° for 1½ hours or until meat thermometer registers 185°. Transfer chicken to a serving platter, and keep warm.

Coat a large nonstick skillet with cooking spray; place over medium-high heat until hot. Add yellow squash, zucchini, tomato, pepper, and shallots; sauté 3 to 4 minutes or until vegetables are crisp-tender. Arrange vegetable mixture around chicken. Yield: 6 servings.

PER SERVING: 175 CALORIES (30% FROM FAT)
FAT 5.9G (SATURATED FAT 1.5G)
PROTEIN 21.8G   CARBOHYDRATE 9.2G
CHOLESTEROL 61MG   SODIUM 170MG

HERBED CHICKEN WITH SOUR CREAM-WINE SAUCE

6 chicken leg quarters (about 3 pounds), skinned
¾ teaspoon dried whole oregano
¾ teaspoon dried whole thyme
½ teaspoon dried whole basil
¼ teaspoon freshly ground black pepper
½ cup Chablis or other dry white wine
½ cup canned low-sodium chicken broth, undiluted
3 tablespoons all-purpose flour
3 tablespoons water
Vegetable cooking spray
1 cup sliced fresh mushrooms
¼ cup shredded carrot
3 tablespoons nonfat sour cream alternative

Place chicken leg quarters in a single layer in a 13- x 9- x 2-inch baking dish. Combine oregano, thyme, basil, and pepper in a small bowl; sprinkle evenly over chicken. Combine wine and broth; pour over chicken. Cover and bake at 350° for 45 minutes. Uncover and bake an additional 15 minutes or until chicken is done.

Transfer chicken to a warm serving platter; keep warm. Transfer cooking juices to a medium saucepan. Combine flour and water to form a smooth paste; stir into cooking juices. Cook over medium heat, stirring constantly, until sauce thickens and bubbles. Remove from heat; keep warm.

Coat a small skillet with cooking spray. Place skillet over medium-high heat until hot; add mushrooms and carrot, and sauté until tender. Stir sautéed vegetables and sour cream into sauce. Spoon sauce evenly over chicken. Yield: 6 servings.

PER SERVING: 204 CALORIES (27% FROM FAT)
FAT 6.2G (SATURATED FAT 1.6G)
PROTEIN 27.2G   CARBOHYDRATE 9.2G
CHOLESTEROL 102MG   SODIUM 118MG

Herbed Chicken with Sour Cream-Wine Sauce

HONEY-BAKED DRUMSTICKS

½ cup regular oats, uncooked
2 tablespoons grated Parmesan cheese
⅛ teaspoon salt
¼ teaspoon paprika
¼ teaspoon pepper
Dash of garlic powder
8 chicken drumsticks, skinned (about
　　1¾ pounds)
2 tablespoons honey
Fresh parsley sprigs (optional)

Combine first 6 ingredients in container of an electric blender or food processor; cover and process until mixture resembles coarse meal.

Brush chicken drumsticks lightly with honey; dredge in oat mixture. Place drumsticks on a rack in a roasting pan. Bake at 400° for 15 minutes. Turn drumsticks, and bake an additional 20 minutes or until chicken is tender and golden. Transfer drumsticks to a large serving platter. Garnish with fresh parsley sprigs, if desired. Yield: 4 servings.

PER SERVING: 240 CALORIES (26% FROM FAT)
FAT 6.8G (SATURATED FAT 2.0G)
PROTEIN 27.9G　CARBOHYDRATE 15.7G
CHOLESTEROL 103MG　SODIUM 228MG

Fat Burner

The top rack of a broiler pan allows fat to drip away from chicken during baking and broiling. For easy cleanup, coat the rack and bottom pan with vegetable cooking spray before placing the chicken on the rack. Lining the bottom pan with aluminum foil or pouring water in the pan to cover the bottom is also helpful.

CRISPY OVEN-FRIED CHICKEN

For a great kid's meal, team either of these "fried" chicken recipes with a green vegetable, fruit salad, and commercial dinner rolls. For dessert, top ½ cup vanilla ice milk with 2 tablespoons frozen, thawed strawberries.

¼ cup plus 2 tablespoons frozen egg substitute,
　　thawed
1 tablespoon water
1 cup crispy rice cereal, crushed
⅓ cup toasted wheat germ
1 tablespoon instant minced onion
½ teaspoon salt-free herb seasoning blend
¼ teaspoon garlic powder
¼ teaspoon salt
¼ teaspoon pepper
1 (3-pound) broiler-fryer, cut up and skinned
¼ cup all-purpose flour
Vegetable cooking spray

Combine egg substitute and water in a shallow dish; stir well. Combine cereal and next 6 ingredients in a shallow dish; stir well.

Place chicken pieces and flour in a large heavy-duty, zip-top plastic bag; seal bag, and shake until chicken is well coated.

Dip chicken in egg substitute mixture; dredge in cereal mixture. Place chicken on rack of a broiler pan coated with cooking spray. Bake, uncovered, at 350° for 1 hour or until chicken is tender and golden. Yield: 6 servings.

PER SERVING: 248 CALORIES (19% FROM FAT)
FAT 5.2G (SATURATED FAT 1.2G)
PROTEIN 34.3G　CARBOHYDRATE 14.0G
CHOLESTEROL 99MG　SODIUM 278MG

Most of the fat content of chicken lies in and just under the skin. Remove the skin and excess fat before cooking to keep Crispy Oven-Fried Chicken as low in fat as possible.

For less mess, combine the flour and chicken in a large heavy-duty, zip-top plastic bag. Seal the bag, and shake it until the chicken is well coated with the flour.

Bake the chicken on the rack of a broiler pan. This allows air to circulate, creating a crisp crust over the entire surface of the chicken rather than just on the top.

Crispy Oven-Fried Chicken

FRUITED CHICKEN THIGHS

6 chicken thighs (2 pounds), skinned
½ cup unsweetened apple juice
½ cup unsweetened orange juice
¼ cup lemon juice
¼ cup raisins
¼ cup chopped dried apricots
¼ cup chopped pitted prunes
¼ teaspoon ground ginger
1 medium onion, thinly sliced and separated
   into rings

Place chicken in a 12- x 8- x 2-inch baking dish. Combine apple juice, orange juice, and lemon juice; pour over chicken. Cover and marinate in refrigerator 2 hours.

Drain chicken, reserving marinade; add raisins, apricots, prunes, and ginger to marinade, stirring well. Arrange onion rings over chicken; pour marinade mixture over chicken. Cover and bake at 350° for 1 hour.

Transfer chicken, onion, and fruit to a serving platter, using a slotted spoon; discard cooking liquid. Yield: 6 servings.

PER SERVING: 216 CALORIES (21% FROM FAT)
FAT 5.1G (SATURATED FAT 1.3G)
PROTEIN 23.7G CARBOHYDRATE 19.0G
CHOLESTEROL 91MG SODIUM 103MG

FYI

Our recipe for Chicken Provençale reflects the strong personality of one of France's great regional cuisines. The spicy Mediterranean taste of Provence typically includes herbs such as basil, thyme, and fennel, as well as garlic and olive oil. Serve with fettuccine, a green salad, and a simple fruit dessert.

CHICKEN PROVENÇALE

¼ teaspoon salt
3 (8-ounce) chicken breast halves, skinned
3 (8-ounce) chicken thighs, skinned
3 (4-ounce) chicken drumsticks, skinned
1 tablespoon olive oil
1½ cups chopped green pepper
½ cup chopped onion
1 clove garlic, minced
1 (1-pound) eggplant, peeled and cut crosswise
   into ¼-inch-thick slices
2 medium tomatoes, peeled and cut crosswise
   into ¼-inch-thick slices
¼ teaspoon salt
¼ cup chopped fresh parsley
2 teaspoons dried whole basil
Fresh basil (optional)

Sprinkle ¼ teaspoon salt over chicken; set aside. Heat oil in a large nonstick skillet over medium heat. Add chicken; cook 5 minutes on each side or until browned. Arrange chicken in a 13- x 9- x 2-inch baking dish; set aside.

Add green pepper, onion, and garlic to skillet; sauté 5 minutes over medium heat. Spoon over chicken. Arrange eggplant over chicken. Top with tomato; sprinkle with ¼ teaspoon salt, parsley, and dried basil. Cover; bake at 375° for 1 hour. Garnish with fresh basil, if desired. Yield: 9 servings.

PER SERVING: 189 CALORIES (26% FROM FAT)
FAT 5.4G (SATURATED FAT 1.2)
PROTEIN 27.6G CARBOHYDRATE 7.0G
CHOLESTEROL 86MG SODIUM 230MG

LEMON-GARLIC CHICKEN

½ cup fine, dry breadcrumbs
2 cloves garlic, minced
¼ teaspoon salt
¼ cup fresh lemon juice
1 tablespoon olive oil
6 (6-ounce) skinned chicken breast halves
Vegetable cooking spray
Lemon wedges (optional)

Combine breadcrumbs, garlic, and salt in a large heavy-duty, zip-top plastic bag, shaking well to combine; set aside.

Combine lemon juice and oil; brush over both sides of chicken. Place chicken in zip-top bag, 1 piece at a time, shaking to coat. Remove chicken from bag, and place in a 12- x 8- x 2-inch baking dish coated with cooking spray. Sprinkle remaining crumbs over chicken.

Bake chicken, uncovered, at 375° for 45 minutes or until done. Serve with lemon wedges, if desired. Yield: 6 servings.

PER SERVING: 208 CALORIES (19% FROM FAT)
FAT 4.4 (SATURATED FAT 0.8G)
PROTEIN 32.8G   CARBOHYDRATE 7.3G
CHOLESTEROL 80MG   SODIUM 248MG

TANGY OVEN-BARBECUED CHICKEN

½ cup jellied cranberry sauce
¼ cup no-salt-added tomato paste
2 tablespoons prepared mustard
1 teaspoon cider vinegar
4 (6-ounce) skinned chicken breast halves

Line an 11- x 7- x 2-inch baking dish with aluminum foil; set aside.

Combine first 4 ingredients in container of an electric blender. Cover and process until mixture is smooth. Brush mixture evenly over both sides of chicken; reserve remaining mixture.

Place chicken, bone side up, in prepared dish. Bake, uncovered, at 375° for 25 minutes. Turn chicken; brush with remaining cranberry mixture. Bake, uncovered, an additional 20 minutes or until chicken is tender. Yield: 4 servings.

PER SERVING: 204 CALORIES (11% FROM FAT)
FAT 2.4G (SATURATED FAT 0.4G)
PROTEIN 27.1G   CARBOHYDRATE 17.3G
CHOLESTEROL 66MG   SODIUM 195MG

CHICKEN WITH MUSHROOM PESTO

1 cup loosely packed fresh basil leaves
¾ cup sliced fresh mushrooms
4 cloves garlic
2 tablespoons nonfat buttermilk
6 (6-ounce) skinned chicken breast halves
Vegetable cooking spray
3 tablespoons low-sodium soy sauce
2 tablespoons honey
½ teaspoon dark sesame oil

Position knife blade in food processor bowl; add first 3 ingredients. Process 3 seconds or until blended. Slowly add nonfat buttermilk through food chute with processor running, blending until mixture forms a paste.

Place 1 chicken breast half, bone side down, on a cutting board; cut lengthwise into side of breast, forming a pocket. Stuff pocket with one-sixth of mushroom mixture. Place chicken, breast side up, on a rack in a roasting pan coated with cooking spray. Repeat procedure with remaining chicken breasts and mushroom mixture.

Combine soy sauce, honey, and sesame oil; brush over chicken. Bake at 400° for 30 minutes or until chicken is tender and golden, basting occasionally. Yield: 6 servings.

PER SERVING: 162 CALORIES (11% FROM FAT)
FAT 2.0G (SATURATED FAT 0.5G)
PROTEIN 26.8G   CARBOHYDRATE 8.3G
CHOLESTEROL 64MG   SODIUM 384MG

Vegetable-Filled Chicken Breasts

VEGETABLE-FILLED CHICKEN BREASTS

6 (4-ounce) skinned, boned chicken breast
   halves
12 small fresh asparagus spears
1 cup plus 2 tablespoons (4½ ounces)
   shredded nonfat mozzarella cheese
¾ cup sliced fresh mushrooms
1 cup frozen artichoke hearts, thawed,
   drained, and chopped
1 tablespoon diced pimiento
¼ teaspoon salt
¼ teaspoon pepper
½ cup frozen egg substitute, thawed
¾ cup fine, dry breadcrumbs
2 tablespoons reduced-calorie margarine
Vegetable cooking spray
Dash of paprika
Fresh chives (optional)

Place chicken between 2 sheets of heavy-duty plastic wrap, and flatten to ¼-inch thickness, using a meat mallet or rolling pin. Set aside.

Snap off tough ends of asparagus. Remove scales from stalks with a knife or vegetable peeler, if desired. Arrange asparagus, cheese, and mushrooms evenly on chicken breast halves. Top evenly with artichoke and pimiento; sprinkle with salt and pepper. Fold chicken over vegetable mixture, and secure with wooden picks. Dip chicken in egg substitute, and dredge in breadcrumbs.

Melt margarine in a large nonstick skillet over medium heat. Add chicken, and cook 6 to 8 minutes on each side or until browned. Remove chicken from skillet, and place on a baking sheet. Coat chicken with cooking spray; sprinkle with paprika. Bake at 350° for 15 to 18 minutes or until golden. Transfer chicken to a serving platter, and remove wooden picks. Garnish with fresh chives, if desired. Yield: 6 servings.

PER SERVING: 248 CALORIES (19% FROM FAT)
FAT 5.2G (SATURATED FAT 0.9G)
PROTEIN 36.1G CARBOHYDRATE 13.5G
CHOLESTEROL 66MG SODIUM 489MG

LEMON CHICKEN CUTLETS

6 (4-ounce) skinned, boned chicken breast
   halves
¼ teaspoon salt
¼ teaspoon pepper
Vegetable cooking spray
1 tablespoon margarine
¼ cup dry sherry
¼ cup chopped onion
2 tablespoons grated lemon rind
2 tablespoons lemon juice
1 cup water
1 teaspoon chicken-flavored bouillon granules
¼ cup water
2 tablespoons all-purpose flour
¼ cup grated Parmesan cheese
¼ teaspoon paprika
2 tablespoons chopped fresh parsley

Place chicken between 2 sheets of heavy-duty plastic wrap; flatten to ¼-inch thickness, using a meat mallet or rolling pin. Sprinkle with salt and pepper; set aside.

Coat a large skillet with cooking spray; add margarine, and place over medium heat until margarine melts. Add chicken to skillet, and cook 3 minutes on each side or until lightly browned. Transfer chicken to a 13- x 9- x 2-inch baking dish coated with cooking spray, reserving liquid in skillet.

Add sherry, onion, lemon rind, and lemon juice to skillet; cook over medium heat 5 minutes or until onion is tender. Add 1 cup water and bouillon granules to skillet. Combine ¼ cup water and flour, stirring well; add to liquid in skillet. Cook over medium heat, stirring constantly, 5 minutes or until thickened and bubbly. Spoon sauce over chicken; sprinkle with Parmesan cheese, paprika, and parsley. Bake at 350° for 15 minutes or until thoroughly heated. Yield: 6 servings.

PER SERVING: 201 CALORIES (28% FROM FAT)
FAT 6.3G (SATURATED FAT 1.9G)
PROTEIN 28.4G CARBOHYDRATE 6.3G
CHOLESTEROL 75MG SODIUM 384MG

CHICKEN MEDAILLONS WITH PEPPER SAUCE

2 cups chopped sweet red pepper
1⅓ cups peeled, diced round red potato
⅔ cup Chablis or other dry white wine
⅔ cup canned no-salt-added chicken broth,
    undiluted
⅛ teaspoon salt
8 (4-ounce) skinned, boned chicken breast
    halves
¾ cup light ricotta cheese
¼ cup light process cream cheese product
2 tablespoons minced fresh basil
2 tablespoons minced fresh oregano
2 tablespoons minced fresh parsley
1 teaspoon minced garlic
½ teaspoon pepper
¼ teaspoon salt
½ teaspoon salt-free lemon-pepper seasoning
Vegetable cooking spray

Combine first 5 ingredients in a medium saucepan; stir well. Bring to a boil; cover, reduce heat, and simmer 20 minutes. Transfer mixture to container of an electric blender; cover and process until smooth. Pour mixture through a wire-mesh strainer into a bowl; discard solids, and set pepper sauce aside.

Place chicken between 2 sheets of heavy-duty plastic wrap, and flatten to ¼-inch thickness, using a meat mallet or rolling pin.

Combine ricotta cheese and next 7 ingredients in a bowl; stir well. Spread cheese mixture over chicken. Roll up jellyroll fashion, starting with short end, tucking ends under. Secure chicken rolls with picks; sprinkle with lemon-pepper seasoning. Place rolls on a baking sheet coated with cooking spray. Bake at 375° for 35 minutes or until chicken is tender and lightly browned. Remove picks; cut chicken rolls into ½-inch slices. Spoon pepper sauce onto individual serving plates. Arrange chicken, cut side down, on sauce. Yield: 8 servings.

PER SERVING: 194 CALORIES (17% FROM FAT)
FAT 3.7G (SATURATED FAT 1.6G)
PROTEIN 30.4G CARBOHYDRATE 9.3G
CHOLESTEROL 73MG SODIUM 245MG

CHICKEN CORDON BLEU

This dish is complemented by seasoned wild and white rice and steamed broccoli. Limit or omit butter in the rice and broccoli if you're watching your calorie and fat intake.

4 (4-ounce) skinned, boned chicken breast
    halves
¼ teaspoon pepper
2 (1-ounce) slices 98% fat-free ham, halved
¾ cup (3 ounces) shredded part-skim
    mozzarella cheese
½ cup cornflakes cereal, crushed
½ teaspoon paprika
¼ teaspoon garlic powder
⅓ cup skim milk
Vegetable cooking spray

Place chicken between 2 sheets of heavy-duty plastic wrap. Flatten to ¼-inch thickness, using a meat mallet or rolling pin. Sprinkle with pepper.

Top each chicken breast half with a piece of ham and 3 tablespoons mozzarella cheese. Roll up jellyroll fashion. Tuck in sides; secure each roll with wooden picks.

Combine cereal, paprika, and garlic powder in a shallow dish. Dip each roll in milk; dredge in cereal mixture. Place in an 11- x 7- x 2-inch baking dish coated with cooking spray. Bake at 350° for 30 minutes or until done. Discard wooden picks. Yield: 4 servings.

PER SERVING: 247 CALORIES (21% FROM FAT)
FAT 5.7G (SATURATED FAT 2.9G)
PROTEIN 35.4G CARBOHYDRATE 11.5G
CHOLESTEROL 85MG SODIUM 398MG

Chicken Cordon Bleu

CHICKEN EN PAPILLOTE

If you don't have parchment paper on hand, you may use aluminum foil instead.

1 pound fresh asparagus spears
4 (4-ounce) skinned, boned chicken breast
    halves
2 small sweet red peppers, cut into julienne
    strips
2 tablespoons low-sodium soy sauce
2 teaspoons peeled, grated gingerroot
2 teaspoons water
2 teaspoons honey
2 teaspoons dark sesame oil
½ teaspoon sesame seeds, toasted
Vegetable cooking spray

Snap off tough ends of asparagus. Remove scales with a knife or a vegetable peeler, if desired. Cut asparagus into 3-inch pieces. Arrange in a vegetable steamer over boiling water; cover and steam 4 minutes or until crisp-tender. Rinse with cold water; drain well.

Place chicken between 2 sheets of heavy-duty plastic wrap, and flatten to ¼-inch thickness, using a meat mallet or rolling pin. Set aside.

Cut 4 (15-inch) squares of parchment paper; fold each square in half. Trim each into a large heart shape. Place parchment hearts on 2 large baking sheets, and open out flat.

Divide asparagus and half of pepper strips evenly among parchment hearts. Place vegetables on half of each parchment heart near the crease. Top each with a chicken breast half and remaining pepper strips. Combine soy sauce, gingerroot, water, honey, and oil in a small bowl, stirring well. Drizzle mixture evenly over chicken and vegetables. Sprinkle evenly with sesame seeds.

Fold over remaining halves of hearts. Fold edges over to seal. Starting with rounded edges of hearts, pleat and crimp edges of parchment to make an airtight seal. Spray packets with cooking spray. Bake at 400° for 12 minutes or until bags are puffed and lightly browned.

Place packets on serving plates. To serve, cut an opening in the top of each packet, and fold paper back. Serve immediately. Yield: 4 servings.

PER SERVING: 190 CALORIES (21% FROM FAT)
FAT 4.4G (SATURATED FAT 0.8G)
PROTEIN 28.7G CARBOHYDRATE 8.6G
CHOLESTEROL 66MG SODIUM 272MG

CHINESE PLUM CHICKEN

Commercial plum sauce makes this dish quick and easy. For a more elegant presentation, serve the chicken over rice.

4 (4-ounce) skinned, boned chicken breast
    halves
¼ cup minced onion
2 tablespoons lemon juice
2 tablespoons low-sodium soy sauce
½ teaspoon dry mustard
¼ teaspoon ground ginger
¼ teaspoon crushed red pepper
1 (8½-ounce) jar commercial plum sauce

Place chicken in an 11- x 7- x 2-inch baking dish. Combine onion and next 6 ingredients; stir well, and pour over chicken.

Bake, uncovered, at 350° for 50 minutes or until chicken is done, basting occasionally with plum sauce mixture. Yield: 4 servings.

PER SERVING: 212 CALORIES (8% FROM FAT)
FAT 1.9G (SATURATED FAT 0.4G)
PROTEIN 27.8G CARBOHYDRATE 21.4G
CHOLESTEROL 66MG SODIUM 318MG

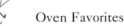

CHICKEN BROCCOLI CASSEROLE

2   tablespoons chopped shallots
½   teaspoon minced garlic
2   tablespoons reduced-calorie margarine,
      melted and divided
¼   cup plus 2 tablespoons all-purpose flour
1½ cups canned no-salt-added chicken broth,
      undiluted and divided
1   cup nonfat sour cream alternative
¼   cup (1 ounce) shredded reduced-fat Gruyère
      cheese
¼   cup grated Parmesan cheese
¼   teaspoon salt
⅛   teaspoon ground white pepper
Vegetable cooking spray
6   cups chopped cooked broccoli
3   cups chopped cooked chicken breast (about
      1½ pounds skinned, boned chicken
      breasts)
¼   cup fine, dry breadcrumbs
2   tablespoons grated Parmesan cheese
2   tablespoons minced fresh parsley

Sauté shallots and garlic in 1 tablespoon margarine in a saucepan over medium-high heat until tender. Combine flour and ½ cup chicken broth; stir well. Add flour mixture and remaining 1 cup chicken broth to saucepan. Cook over medium heat, stirring constantly, until mixture is thickened. Remove from heat; add sour cream and next 4 ingredients.

Spread ½ cup sour cream mixture in an 11- x 7- x 1½-inch baking dish coated with cooking spray. Add broccoli and 1¼ cups sour cream mixture. Top with chicken and remaining sour cream mixture.

Combine breadcrumbs, 2 tablespoons Parmesan cheese, parsley, and remaining 1 tablespoon margarine; stir well. Sprinkle evenly over top of casserole. Bake, uncovered, at 350° for 30 minutes or until thoroughly heated. Yield: 8 servings.

PER SERVING: 208 CALORIES (25% FROM FAT)
FAT 5.8G (SATURATED FAT 1.8G)
PROTEIN 23.6G   CARBOHYDRATE 14.2G
CHOLESTEROL 47MG   SODIUM 288MG

CHICKEN LINGUINE

(pictured on page 78)

1   pound sliced fresh mushrooms
½   cup dry sherry
2   tablespoons reduced-calorie margarine,
      melted and divided
4   (4-ounce) skinned, boned chicken breast
      halves
Vegetable cooking spray
½   cup chopped onion
¼   cup plus 2 tablespoons all-purpose flour
3   cups canned no-salt-added chicken broth,
      undiluted and divided
1   (8-ounce) carton nonfat sour cream
      alternative
1   (16-ounce) package linguine, uncooked
½   cup (2 ounces) shredded reduced-fat
      Monterey Jack cheese
¼   cup plus 2 tablespoons freshly grated
      Parmesan cheese, divided
⅛   teaspoon freshly ground black pepper
¼   cup fine, dry breadcrumbs

Sauté mushrooms in sherry and 1 tablespoon margarine in a nonstick skillet over high heat 5 minutes. Place chicken in a saucepan; add water to cover. Bring to a boil; cover, reduce heat, and simmer 20 minutes. Drain; let cool and shred.

Coat a saucepan with cooking spray; add onion, and sauté over medium heat until tender. Combine flour and ½ cup canned broth. Add remaining 2½ cups broth and flour mixture to onion. Cook over medium heat until thickened. Remove from heat; stir in sour cream.

Cook linguine, omitting salt and fat; drain. Combine mushrooms, chicken, sour cream mixture, Monterey Jack cheese, ¼ cup Parmesan cheese, and pepper. Stir in linguine. Spoon into a 13- x 9- x 2-inch baking dish coated with cooking spray.

Combine breadcrumbs, remaining 2 tablespoons Parmesan cheese, and remaining 1 tablespoon margarine; sprinkle over chicken. Bake, uncovered, at 350° for 30 minutes. Yield: 12 servings.

PER SERVING: 289 CALORIES (19% FROM FAT)
FAT 6.1G (SATURATED FAT 2.0G)
PROTEIN 18.7G   CARBOHYDRATE 37.7G
CHOLESTEROL 31MG   SODIUM 167MG

Chicken Divan

CHICKEN DIVAN

2 (10-ounce) packages frozen broccoli spears, thawed
3 cups chopped cooked chicken breast (about 1½ pounds skinned, boned chicken breasts)
½ cup (2 ounces) shredded reduced-fat sharp Cheddar cheese
1¼ cups skim milk
1 (10¾-ounce) can one-third-less-salt cream of mushroom soup, undiluted
1 teaspoon lemon juice
⅛ teaspoon salt
⅛ teaspoon pepper
3 tablespoons all-purpose flour
3 tablespoons water
½ cup finely crushed onion-flavored melba toast rounds (about 19)
1 tablespoon margarine, melted
3 sweet red pepper rings (optional)
Fresh parsley sprigs (optional)

In a 13- x 9- x 2-inch baking dish, arrange broccoli spears horizontally in 2 rows, with stalks facing each other in center of dish. Spoon chicken on top of stalk ends, and top with cheese; set aside.

Combine milk, soup, lemon juice, salt, and pepper in a heavy saucepan; stir well. Combine flour and water in a bowl; stir well. Add to soup mixture; stir well. Bring to a boil over medium heat, stirring constantly with a wire whisk. Cook 8 minutes or until thickened and bubbly, stirring constantly; pour evenly over chicken. Combine melba toast crumbs and margarine in a bowl; sprinkle over soup mixture. Garnish with pepper rings, if desired.

Cover and bake at 350° for 20 minutes. Uncover; bake an additional 15 minutes or until thoroughly heated. Let stand 10 minutes before serving. Garnish with parsley, if desired. Yield: 6 servings.

PER SERVING: 378 CALORIES (30% FROM FAT)
FAT 12.7G (SATURATED FAT 3.7G)
PROTEIN 44.9G   CARBOHYDRATE 20.5G
CHOLESTEROL 104MG   SODIUM 766MG

CHICKEN CHILES RELLENOS

3 (4-ounce) cans whole green chiles, drained
1 (4-ounce) can chopped green chiles, drained
2 cups seeded, chopped tomato
2 tablespoons minced green onions
1 tablespoon chopped fresh cilantro
1 tablespoon white wine vinegar
Vegetable cooking spray
½ cup chopped onion
2 cloves garlic, minced
1½ cups chopped cooked chicken breast
½ cup (2 ounces) shredded reduced-fat Monterey Jack cheese
¼ teaspoon salt
¼ teaspoon pepper
2 tablespoons reduced-calorie mayonnaise
1 teaspoon water
1⅓ cups soft French bread crumbs, toasted
Fresh cilantro sprigs (optional)

Reserve 8 whole chiles; chop remaining whole chiles. Combine chopped whole chiles, drained chopped chiles, and next 4 ingredients; stir well. Cover and chill thoroughly.

Coat a large nonstick skillet with cooking spray; place over medium-high heat until hot. Add onion and garlic; sauté until tender. Remove from heat, and let cool slightly. Stir in chicken, cheese, salt, and pepper. Spoon ¼ cup chicken mixture into each whole chile.

Combine mayonnaise and water in a small bowl; stir well. Dip stuffed chiles in mayonnaise mixture, and dredge in bread crumbs. Place on a baking sheet coated with cooking spray. Bake at 450° for 10 to 12 minutes or until golden brown. Serve with chilled tomato mixture. Garnish with fresh cilantro sprigs, if desired. Yield: 4 servings.

PER SERVING: 251 CALORIES (27% FROM FAT)
FAT 7.4G (SATURATED FAT 2.5G)
PROTEIN 21.8G   CARBOHYDRATE 22.5G
CHOLESTEROL 52MG   SODIUM 564MG

Tomatillo Chicken Bake

TOMATILLO CHICKEN BAKE

4 (6-ounce) skinned chicken breast halves
6 fresh tomatillos
Vegetable cooking spray
¾ cup chopped onion
½ cup water
4 cloves garlic, halved
½ teaspoon chicken-flavored
    bouillon granules
1 cup loosely packed fresh cilantro
2 cups sliced fresh mushrooms

¾ cup nonfat sour cream alternative
¾ teaspoon chili powder
½ teaspoon ground cumin
½ teaspoon pepper
¼ teaspoon salt
1 cup (4 ounces) shredded reduced-fat sharp
    Cheddar cheese
6 (6-inch) corn tortillas, each cut into 8 wedges
Tomato wedges (optional)
Fresh cilantro sprigs (optional)

Place chicken in a large Dutch oven; add water to cover. Bring to a boil; cover, reduce heat, and simmer 35 minutes or until chicken is tender. Remove chicken from broth, and let cool slightly. Bone and shred chicken; set aside. Reserve broth for another use.

Remove and discard husks from tomatillos; thinly slice tomatillos. Coat a large skillet with cooking spray; place over medium-high heat until hot. Add tomatillos, and sauté until tender. Remove from skillet, and let cool slightly. Set aside.

Combine onion, ½ cup water, garlic, and bouillon granules in skillet; cook over high heat until liquid evaporates (about 5 minutes).

Combine sautéed tomatillos, onion mixture, and 1 cup fresh cilantro in container of an electric blender or food processor; cover and process until mixture is smooth.

Coat skillet with cooking spray; place over medium-high heat until hot. Add mushrooms; sauté until tender. Remove from heat; stir in shredded chicken, sour cream alternative, and next 4 ingredients. Set aside; keep warm.

Spoon half of tomatillo mixture evenly into 6 individual oven-proof dishes coated with cooking spray. Sprinkle evenly with ⅓ cup cheese; top each with ¼ cup chicken mixture. Repeat procedure with remaining tomatillo mixture, ⅓ cup cheese, and remaining chicken mixture. Sprinkle with remaining ⅓ cup cheese. Arrange 8 tortilla wedges around edges of each dish. Cover and bake at 350° for 15 minutes. Uncover and bake 10 minutes or until thoroughly heated. Garnish each dish with tomato wedges and cilantro sprigs, if desired. Yield: 6 servings.

PER SERVING: 261 CALORIES (26% FROM FAT)
FAT 7.4G (SATURATED FAT 0.7G)
PROTEIN 27.6G   CARBOHYDRATE 20.4G
CHOLESTEROL 59MG   SODIUM 425MG

CHICKEN EMPANADAS

1 cup finely chopped cooked chicken breast
1 (4-ounce) can chopped green chiles, drained
½ cup 1% low-fat cottage cheese
¼ cup (1 ounce) shredded reduced-fat
   Monterey Jack cheese
¾ cup all-purpose flour
¼ cup cornmeal
¼ teaspoon ground red pepper
3 tablespoons reduced-calorie margarine
¼ cup cold water
1 tablespoon all-purpose flour
Vegetable cooking spray
2 teaspoons skim milk
2 teaspoons cornmeal

Combine first 4 ingredients in a medium bowl; stir well. Set aside.

Combine ¾ cup flour, ¼ cup cornmeal, and red pepper in a large bowl; cut in margarine with a pastry blender until mixture resembles coarse meal. Sprinkle cold water, 1 tablespoon at a time, evenly over surface of mixture; stir with a fork until dry ingredients are moistened. Shape into a ball; cover and chill 10 minutes.

Sprinkle 1 tablespoon flour evenly over work surface. Divide dough into fourths; roll each portion to a 5-inch circle on floured surface. Place circles on a baking sheet coated with cooking spray. Spoon ½ cup chicken mixture on one-half of each pastry circle. To seal, fold circles in half, making sure edges are even. Press edges of filled pastry firmly together with a fork. Brush tops with milk, and sprinkle with 2 teaspoons cornmeal. Bake, uncovered, at 400° for 20 minutes or until lightly browned. Let stand 10 minutes. Yield: 4 servings.

PER SERVING: 286 CALORIES (29% FROM FAT)
FAT 9.3G (SATURATED FAT 2.2G)
PROTEIN 22.2G   CARBOHYDRATE 27.6G
CHOLESTEROL 42MG   SODIUM 290MG

LIGHT ENCHILADAS

Vegetable cooking spray
1 pound skinned, boned chicken breasts, cut
    into bite-size pieces
¾ cup chopped onion
1 sweet red pepper, seeded and chopped
1 large green pepper, seeded and chopped
1½ tablespoons chopped fresh cilantro
2 (16-ounce) cans pinto beans, drained and
    mashed
1 (14½-ounce) can no-salt-added tomatoes,
    undrained and chopped
1 (8-ounce) can no-salt-added tomato sauce
1 (4-ounce) can chopped green chiles, drained
¼ teaspoon pepper
10 (8-inch) flour tortillas
¾ cup (3 ounces) shredded reduced-fat
    Monterey Jack cheese

Coat a nonstick skillet with cooking spray; place
over medium-high heat until hot. Add chicken;
sauté 2 minutes or until lightly browned. Add
onion and next 3 ingredients; sauté 3 minutes or
until chicken is done. Remove from heat. Add
beans; stir.

Combine tomato and next 3 ingredients in a
bowl; stir. Spoon ⅓ cup tomato mixture into a 13- x
9- x 2-inch baking dish coated with cooking spray.
Set remaining tomato mixture aside.

Place a damp paper towel in center of a sheet of
aluminum foil. Stack tortillas on paper towel. Cover
stack with another damp paper towel; seal foil.
Bake at 250° for 10 minutes. Spoon chicken mixture evenly down centers of tortillas. Roll tortillas;
place, seam side down, in prepared dish. Pour
remaining tomato mixture over tortillas.

Cover and bake at 350° for 30 minutes or until
thoroughly heated. Uncover and sprinkle with
cheese. Bake 5 minutes or until cheese melts.
Yield: 10 enchiladas.

PER ENCHILADA: 265 CALORIES (21% FROM FAT)
FAT 6.1G (SATURATED FAT 2.2G)
PROTEIN 18.9G CARBOHYDRATE 33.3G
CHOLESTEROL 33MG SODIUM 455MG

CHICKEN-VEGETABLE STRUDEL

*Top steamed asparagus with lemon juice, diced
pimiento, and a sprinkling of blue cheese to serve
alongside this elegant luncheon entrée.*

½ cup diced carrot
½ cup diced sweet red pepper
¼ cup unsweetened orange juice
Butter-flavored vegetable cooking spray
2 cups chopped fresh mushrooms
¼ cup chopped green onions
2 cups shredded cooked chicken breast
1 tablespoon Dijon mustard
½ teaspoon dried whole basil
¼ teaspoon grated orange rind
¼ teaspoon salt
¼ teaspoon pepper
6 sheets commercial frozen phyllo pastry,
    thawed
1 tablespoon fine, dry breadcrumbs
Fresh basil sprigs (optional)

Combine carrot, sweet red pepper, and orange
juice in a small saucepan. Bring to a boil; cover,
reduce heat, and cook 5 to 7 minutes or until crisp-
tender. Drain well. Place vegetables in a medium
bowl, and set aside.

Coat a large nonstick skillet with cooking spray;
place over medium-high heat until hot. Add mushrooms and green onions; sauté until tender. Add
mushroom mixture, shredded chicken, and next 5
ingredients to carrot mixture; stir well to combine.

Place 1 sheet phyllo pastry on a damp towel
(keep remaining phyllo covered). Lightly coat
phyllo with vegetable cooking spray. Layer remaining 5 sheets phyllo on first sheet, lightly coating
each sheet with cooking spray.

Spoon chicken mixture lengthwise down half of
phyllo stack, leaving a ½-inch margin. Roll up
phyllo, jellyroll fashion, starting with long side con-
taining chicken mixture. Tuck ends under; place
diagonally, seam side down, on a baking sheet coated with cooking spray. Lightly coat top of pastry

Chicken-Vegetable Strudel

with cooking spray, and sprinkle with breadcrumbs. Make 11 (¼-inch-deep) slits across top of pastry, using a sharp knife. Bake at 375° for 20 minutes or until golden. Let stand 5 minutes before serving. Transfer to a serving platter and slice. Garnish with fresh basil sprigs, if desired. Yield: 6 servings.

PER SERVING: 182 CALORIES (27% FROM FAT)
FAT 5.4G (SATURATED FAT 1.2G)
PROTEIN 16.1G CARBOHYDRATE 16.4G
CHOLESTEROL 42MG SODIUM 330MG

FYI

How do you handle phyllo dough? No problem, if you follow these tips. Thaw frozen phyllo thoroughly so it won't crumble while assembling. Work on a dry surface with one sheet of phyllo at a time. Keep remaining sheets covered with a damp—not wet—cotton towel to prevent the pastry from drying out. Unused phyllo can be wrapped tightly in plastic wrap and frozen.

Chicken Pot Pie

CHICKEN POT PIE

1 cup all-purpose flour
¼ teaspoon salt
¼ cup shortening
3 tablespoons plus 1 teaspoon ice water
2 (10½-ounce) cans low-sodium chicken broth
2 cups diced unpeeled round red potato
1 cup thinly sliced carrot
½ cup chopped onion
½ cup frozen English peas
¼ cup all-purpose flour
½ teaspoon salt
¼ to ½ teaspoon poultry seasoning
¼ teaspoon pepper
½ cup skim milk
2 cups chopped cooked chicken breast
Butter-flavored vegetable cooking spray

Combine 1 cup flour and ¼ teaspoon salt in a bowl; cut in shortening with a pastry blender until mixture resembles coarse meal. Sprinkle ice water, 1 tablespoon at a time, over surface; toss with a fork until dry ingredients are moistened. Gently press dough into a 4-inch circle on heavy-duty plastic wrap. Cover with wrap; chill 30 minutes.

Bring broth to a boil in a large saucepan over medium-high heat. Add potato; cover and cook 5 minutes. Add carrot and onion; cover and cook 3 minutes. Add peas; cover and cook an additional 2 minutes or until vegetables are tender.

Combine ¼ cup flour, ½ teaspoon salt, poultry seasoning, pepper, and milk in a bowl; stir well. Gradually add to vegetable mixture, stirring well. Cook over medium heat 3 minutes or until thickened and bubbly, stirring constantly. Remove from heat; stir in chicken. Spoon into a 2-quart casserole.

Roll dough, still covered, to a size 1 inch larger than diameter of casserole. Remove plastic wrap; place dough on top of chicken mixture. Fold edges under and flute; cut several slits in top of dough to allow steam to escape. Lightly coat top with cooking spray. Bake at 350° for 55 minutes. Let stand 10 minutes. Yield: 8 servings.

PER SERVING: 273 CALORIES (25% FROM FAT)
FAT 7.7G (SATURATED FAT 2.0G)
PROTEIN 22.0G CARBOHYDRATE 26.9G
CHOLESTEROL 49MG SODIUM 290MG

CHICKEN-DRESSING CASSEROLE

1 cup stone-ground cornmeal
1 teaspoon baking soda
½ teaspoon baking powder
1 cup nonfat buttermilk
¼ cup frozen egg substitute, thawed
Vegetable cooking spray
2 cups chopped cooked chicken
¾ cup chopped onion
¾ cup chopped celery
¾ teaspoon poultry seasoning
½ teaspoon pepper
½ teaspoon rubbed sage
¼ teaspoon salt
Dash of hot sauce
2½ cups canned low-sodium chicken broth
½ cup frozen egg substitute, thawed

Combine cornmeal, baking soda, and baking powder in a bowl; make a well in center of mixture. Combine buttermilk and ¼ cup egg substitute; add buttermilk mixture to dry ingredients, stirring just until dry ingredients are moistened.

Spoon batter into an 8-inch cast-iron skillet coated with cooking spray. Bake at 400° for 20 minutes or until golden. Remove cornbread from skillet, and cool slightly on a wire rack.

Crumble cooled cornbread into a large bowl. Add chicken and remaining ingredients, stirring well. Spoon mixture into a 2-quart baking dish coated with cooking spray. Bake, uncovered, at 350° for 1½ hours. Yield: 6 servings.

PER SERVING: 243 CALORIES (23% FROM FAT)
FAT 6.3G (SATURATED FAT 1.6G)
PROTEIN 24.9G CARBOHYDRATE 21.6G
CHOLESTEROL 55MG SODIUM 454MG

HOT OFF THE STOVETOP

*I*t seems frying used to be chicken's only fate. But with the advent of light cooking, the stovetop calls for different action: poaching, braising, and steaming. We've included traditional favorites such as Chicken Jambalaya and Coq au Vin (page 108). And when you're on the run, count on our ideas for transforming boned chicken breast halves into Chicken Piccata (page 113) and other savory dishes. Then dust off that wok for stir-frying, another favorite low-fat cooking method.

Chicken Jambalaya (Recipe follows on page 118)

Arroz con Pollo

Arroz con Pollo

Serve this Spanish-inspired dish with fresh spinach salad and crusty bread.

Vegetable cooking spray
1 teaspoon vegetable oil
1 (3½-pound) broiler-fryer, cut up and skinned
2 cups water
1 (14½-ounce) can no-salt-added stewed tomatoes, undrained and chopped
1 cup chopped onion
2 teaspoons chicken-flavored bouillon granules
1 clove garlic, minced
1 medium-size jalapeño pepper, minced
¼ teaspoon ground saffron
⅛ teaspoon pepper
1 cup long-grain rice, uncooked
¼ cup sliced pimiento-stuffed olives, drained
2 tablespoons lime juice

Coat a 12-inch skillet with cooking spray; add oil, and place over medium-high heat until hot. Add chicken, and cook 4 minutes on each side or until browned. Remove chicken; drain on paper towels.

Wipe skillet with a paper towel; recoat with cooking spray. Add chicken to skillet with water and next 7 ingredients. Cover and cook over medium heat 15 minutes.

Add rice to skillet; cover and cook over medium heat 20 minutes or until chicken is tender and liquid is absorbed. Remove from heat, and stir in olives; sprinkle with lime juice. Yield: 6 servings.

PER SERVING: 394 CALORIES (24% FROM FAT)
FAT 10.7G (SATURATED FAT 2.8G)
PROTEIN 38.0G CARBOHYDRATE 34.7G
CHOLESTEROL 106MG SODIUM 434MG

FYI

Arroz con Pollo gained fame in this country when Ricky Ricardo claimed it to be his favorite food on the "I Love Lucy" show.

Chicken Fricassee

1 (3-pound) broiler-fryer, cut up and skinned
½ teaspoon freshly ground black pepper
¼ teaspoon salt
1 teaspoon dried whole thyme
Vegetable cooking spray
1 teaspoon vegetable oil
12 small boiling onions
3 cups canned no-salt-added chicken broth, undiluted and divided
1 cup Chablis or other dry white wine
1 pound small fresh mushrooms, sliced
2 teaspoons minced garlic
¼ cup all-purpose flour
1 cup nonfat sour cream alternative
¼ teaspoon ground white pepper
⅛ teaspoon salt
1 tablespoon minced fresh parsley

Sprinkle chicken with ½ teaspoon pepper, ¼ teaspoon salt, and thyme. Coat a Dutch oven with cooking spray; add oil. Place over medium heat until hot. Add chicken and onions; cook until chicken is browned on all sides. Remove chicken, and set aside.

Add 2¾ cups chicken broth and wine to Dutch oven; bring to a boil. Cover, reduce heat, and simmer 15 minutes. Return chicken to pan; cover and simmer 10 minutes or until chicken is tender.

Coat a large nonstick skillet with cooking spray; place over medium-high heat until hot. Add mushrooms, and sauté until tender. Add garlic, and sauté 1 minute.

Combine remaining ¼ cup broth and flour, stirring with a wire whisk until smooth. Gradually add to chicken mixture, stirring well. Stir in mushroom mixture, sour cream, white pepper, and ⅛ teaspoon salt. Cook over low heat 5 minutes or until thoroughly heated, stirring frequently. Sprinkle with parsley. Yield: 6 servings.

PER SERVING: 232 CALORIES (18% FROM FAT)
FAT 4.6G (SATURATED FAT 1.1G)
PROTEIN 28.8G CARBOHYDRATE 16.0G
CHOLESTEROL 76MG SODIUM 268MG

Braised Chicken with Garlic and Spinach

BRAISED CHICKEN WITH GARLIC AND SPINACH

½ pound fresh spinach
1 tablespoon olive oil
3 chicken breast halves (about 1½ pounds), skinned
3 chicken thighs (about ¾ pound), skinned
3 chicken drumsticks (about ½ pound), skinned
¾ cup diagonally sliced carrot
10 cloves garlic, halved
½ cup canned no-salt-added chicken broth, undiluted
¼ teaspoon salt
¼ teaspoon pepper

Remove stems from spinach; wash leaves, and tear into bite-size pieces. Set spinach aside.

Heat oil in a large nonstick skillet over medium heat until hot. Add chicken pieces, and cook 5 minutes on each side or until browned; add carrot and garlic. Cover, reduce heat, and cook 20 minutes, turning chicken once. Remove chicken and carrot from skillet with a slotted spoon; set aside, and keep warm.

Cover and cook garlic an additional 3 minutes. Add broth, salt, and pepper; bring to a boil. Cook, uncovered, 3 minutes or until reduced to ¼ cup. Place mixture in container of an electric blender or food processor; cover and process 30 seconds or until smooth. Set aside.

Place a large Dutch oven over medium heat, and add spinach; cover and cook 3 minutes. (Do not add water.) Drain well.

Place spinach on a serving platter. Arrange chicken and carrot on top of spinach; drizzle with garlic mixture. Yield: 6 servings.

PER SERVING: 185 CALORIES (27% FROM FAT)
FAT 5.5G (SATURATED FAT 1.1G)
PROTEIN 28.0G   CARBOHYDRATE 4.6G
CHOLESTEROL 86MG   SODIUM 228MG

BRAISED CHICKEN OVER COUSCOUS

1 tablespoon seasoned breadcrumbs
2 (4-ounce) skinned, boned chicken thighs
Vegetable cooking spray
1 teaspoon olive oil
½ cup chopped onion
½ cup diced carrot
½ cup diced celery
2 tablespoons water
1 cup canned, undrained diced tomatoes
½ teaspoon grated orange rind
¼ teaspoon dried whole rosemary
⅛ teaspoon salt
⅛ teaspoon coarsely ground pepper
1 clove garlic, crushed
2 cups cooked couscous (cooked without salt or fat)

Place breadcrumbs in a shallow dish; dredge chicken in breadcrumbs, and set aside. Coat a nonstick skillet with cooking spray; add oil. Place over medium-high heat until hot. Add chicken; cook 3 minutes on each side or until browned. Remove chicken from skillet; set aside, and keep warm.

Add onion and next 3 ingredients to skillet; cook over medium heat 5 minutes. Add tomatoes and next 5 ingredients, stirring well. Return chicken to skillet. Cover, reduce heat, and simmer 20 minutes or until chicken is done. Serve chicken mixture over couscous. Yield: 2 servings.

PER SERVING: 433 CALORIES (16% FROM FAT)
FAT 7.6G (SATURATED FAT 1.5G)
PROTEIN 32.3G   CARBOHYDRATE 58.4G
CHOLESTEROL 94MG   SODIUM 569MG

COQ AU VIN

This classic French dish combines chicken and red wine. Serve it with seasoned rice, spinach salad, and crusty loaves of bread.

Vegetable cooking spray
1 tablespoon olive oil, divided
5 chicken thighs (about 1¼ pounds), skinned
5 chicken drumsticks (about 1¼ pounds), skinned
1 cup chopped onion
2 cloves garlic, minced
¾ cup Burgundy or other dry red wine
¼ cup brandy
1 cup canned low-sodium chicken broth, undiluted
2 tablespoons tomato paste
½ teaspoon dried whole thyme
½ teaspoon salt
¼ teaspoon pepper
3 cups fresh mushrooms, halved lengthwise
2 cups (½-inch) sliced carrot
2 tablespoons cornstarch
2 tablespoons water

Coat a 6-quart pressure cooker with cooking spray; add 1½ teaspoons oil. Place over medium heat until hot. Add thighs; cook 2 minutes, browning on all sides. Remove from cooker. Repeat procedure with remaining 1½ teaspoons oil and drumsticks; set aside. Add onion and garlic to cooker; sauté until tender. Stir in wine, brandy, and broth, scraping up browned bits on bottom of cooker. Add tomato paste and next 5 ingredients; stir well. Return thighs and drumsticks to cooker, spooning broth mixture over chicken.

Close lid securely; bring to high pressure over high heat (about 7 minutes). Reduce heat to medium-high or level needed to maintain high pressure; cook 9 minutes. Remove from heat, and cool under cold, running water. Remove lid; place chicken on a serving platter. Combine cornstarch and water, stirring well. Add to broth mixture in pan; stir well. Bring to a boil, and cook 1 minute, stirring constantly. Pour over chicken. Yield: 5 servings.

Note: Recipe may be prepared in a Dutch oven. After adding tomato paste and next 5 ingredients, return chicken thighs and drumsticks to Dutch oven. Bring mixture to a boil; cover, reduce heat, and simmer 1 hour or until chicken is tender. (Additional liquid may be added, if desired.) Proceed as directed above.

PER SERVING: 348 CALORIES (26% FROM FAT)
FAT 10.0G (SATURATED FAT 2.1G)
PROTEIN 36.4G   CARBOHYDRATE 14.6G
CHOLESTEROL 131MG   SODIUM 421MG

Always follow manufacturer's instructions for your pressure cooker. According to general guidelines, put the lid on the pressure cooker, and lock it in place.

Place the pressure regulator on the vent pipe. Bring the cooker up to pressure over high heat; the pressure regulator will rock vigorously. Adjust heat to maintain high pressure.

Lower pressure inside the cooker by placing it under cold running water or letting it stand 10 minutes to drop naturally.

Coq au Vin

CHICKEN CACCIATORE

1 small onion, chopped
¼ cup water
1 cup canned whole tomatoes, undrained and
  chopped
½ cup tomato puree
1 teaspoon dried whole oregano
½ teaspoon garlic powder
⅛ teaspoon pepper
4 (8-ounce) skinned chicken breast halves
2 cups cooked spaghetti (cooked without salt
  or fat)

Combine onion and water in a 10-inch skillet; cover and cook over medium heat 3 to 4 minutes or until onion is tender. Stir in tomato, tomato puree, and seasonings. Cover, reduce heat, and simmer 10 minutes.

Add chicken to skillet; spoon tomato mixture over chicken. Cover and simmer 30 minutes; uncover and simmer an additional 15 minutes. Serve over spaghetti. Yield: 4 servings.

PER SERVING: 266 CALORIES (7% FROM FAT)
FAT 2.2G (SATURATED FAT 0.5G)
PROTEIN 31.7G CARBOHYDRATE 29.1G
CHOLESTEROL 67MG SODIUM 300MG

FYI

It is important to check chicken for doneness. Slash the thickest part of the meat—it should no longer look pink. For a more accurate test, insert a meat thermometer into the thickest part of the chicken (usually the thigh on a whole broiler-fryer). The thermometer should reach a temperature of 180°. Boneless parts should be cooked to an internal temperature of 160°.

APPLE-KISSED CHICKEN

½ cup unsweetened apple juice
3 tablespoons apple butter
1 teaspoon grated lemon rind
1 tablespoon lemon juice
6 (6-ounce) skinned chicken breast halves
½ teaspoon poultry seasoning
Vegetable cooking spray
1 small onion, thinly sliced
1 small cooking apple, cored and cut into
  12 wedges
1 tablespoon plus 1 teaspoon cornstarch
1 tablespoon plus 1 teaspoon water
2 tablespoons chopped walnuts, toasted
Apple wedges (optional)
Fresh sage sprigs (optional)

Combine first 4 ingredients in a small bowl; stir well. Set aside.

Sprinkle chicken with poultry seasoning. Coat a large nonstick skillet with cooking spray; place over medium-high heat until hot. Add chicken, and cook 5 minutes on each side or until browned. Remove chicken; drain on paper towels. Wipe drippings from skillet with a paper towel. Return chicken to skillet. Pour apple juice mixture over chicken, and top with onion slices. Cover, reduce heat, and simmer 10 minutes. Add apple wedges. Cover and simmer 12 minutes or until chicken is tender.

Transfer chicken and apple wedges to a serving platter, using a slotted spoon. Dissolve cornstarch in water in a small bowl. Add to apple juice mixture in skillet, stirring constantly. Cook over medium heat, stirring constantly, until mixture is thickened. Spoon sauce over chicken, and sprinkle with walnuts. If desired, garnish with apple wedges and fresh sage sprigs. Yield: 6 servings.

PER SERVING: 228 CALORIES (22% FROM FAT)
FAT 5.5G (SATURATED FAT 1.1G)
PROTEIN 29.8G CARBOHYDRATE 13.9G
CHOLESTEROL 78MG SODIUM 70MG

Taco-Tico Chicken

TACO-TICO CHICKEN

½ teaspoon chili powder
¼ teaspoon ground cumin
⅛ teaspoon garlic powder
⅛ teaspoon ground red pepper
6 (6-ounce) skinned chicken breast halves
Vegetable cooking spray
1 teaspoon vegetable oil
1 (14½-ounce) can no-salt-added whole
    tomatoes, undrained and chopped
½ cup sliced green onions
¼ cup sliced ripe olives
1 tablespoon golden tequila
1 teaspoon seeded, chopped jalapeño pepper
2 teaspoons cornstarch
2 tablespoons water
¼ cup plus 2 tablespoons low-fat sour cream
¼ cup (1 ounce) shredded 40% less-fat
    Cheddar cheese
2 tablespoons chopped fresh cilantro

Combine first 4 ingredients; sprinkle over both sides of chicken. Coat a large nonstick skillet with cooking spray; add oil. Place over medium-high heat until hot. Add chicken; cook 2 minutes on each side or until browned. Remove chicken from skillet. Drain and pat dry with paper towels. Wipe drippings from skillet with a paper towel.

Return chicken to skillet. Add tomato and next 4 ingredients. Bring to a boil; cover, reduce heat, and simmer 20 minutes or until tender. Transfer chicken to a serving platter, using a slotted spoon.

Combine cornstarch and water; stir well. Add to tomato mixture; bring to a boil. Cook 1 minute or until slightly thickened, stirring constantly. Spoon over chicken; top with sour cream, cheese, and cilantro. Yield: 6 servings.

PER SERVING: 207 CALORIES (30% FROM FAT)
FAT 6.8G (SATURATED FAT 2.6G)
PROTEIN 27.8G CARBOHYDRATE 8.0G
CHOLESTEROL 78MG SODIUM 155MG

CHICKEN WITH GARLIC AND TOMATO

2 cups peeled, coarsely chopped tomato
1 cup red wine vinegar
¾ cup canned low-sodium chicken broth, undiluted
2 tablespoons no-salt-added tomato paste
15 cloves garlic
4 (6-ounce) skinned chicken breast halves
1 teaspoon fines herbes
1 bay leaf
Fresh thyme sprigs (optional)
Fresh oregano sprigs (optional)

Combine first 5 ingredients in a medium saucepan; stir well. Cover and simmer mixture over medium-low heat 20 minutes. Add chicken, fines herbes, and bay leaf. Cover and simmer an additional 25 minutes or until chicken is tender.

Transfer chicken to a serving platter, and keep warm. Bring tomato mixture to a boil; cook, uncovered, over medium heat 20 minutes or until mixture is reduced to 1⅓ cups. Remove and discard bay leaf. Remove and discard garlic, if desired. Spoon tomato mixture over chicken. If desired, garnish chicken with fresh thyme and oregano sprigs. Yield: 4 servings.

PER SERVING: 183 CALORIES (10% FROM FAT)
FAT 2.1G (SATURATED FAT 0.5G)
PROTEIN 28.5G CARBOHYDRATE 12.4G
CHOLESTEROL 66MG SODIUM 102MG

Chicken with Garlic and Tomato

CHICKEN PICCATA

4 (4-ounce) skinned, boned chicken breast
  halves
3 tablespoons all-purpose flour
1 teaspoon paprika
Vegetable cooking spray
1 tablespoon margarine
2 tablespoons Chablis or other dry white wine
2 tablespoons lemon juice
¼ teaspoon chicken-flavored bouillon granules
Lemon slices (optional)
Fresh parsley sprigs (optional)

Place chicken between 2 sheets of heavy-duty
plastic wrap, and flatten to ¼-inch thickness, using
a meat mallet or rolling pin. Combine flour and
paprika in a shallow container; dredge chicken
breast halves in flour mixture.

Coat a large nonaluminum skillet with cooking
spray; add margarine, and place over medium-high
heat until margarine melts. Add chicken, and cook
5 minutes on each side or until chicken is done.
Remove from skillet, and keep warm.

Add wine, lemon juice, and bouillon granules to
skillet, and cook 30 seconds, stirring constantly.
Pour over chicken breasts; garnish with lemon
slices and parsley, if desired. Yield: 4 servings.

PER SERVING: 182 CALORIES (23% FROM FAT)
FAT 4.6G (SATURATED FAT 1.0G)
PROTEIN 27.0G CARBOHYDRATE 5.6G
CHOLESTEROL 66MG SODIUM 156MG

Quick Tip

Boned chicken breast halves cook in a skillet in 10 minutes or less. They cook even
more quickly when cut into strips or cubes for
stir-frying. When pounded thin, boned chick-
en breasts can be stuffed. Keep some in your
freezer for a last minute meal. (See instructions for thawing frozen chicken on page 8.)

HONEY CHICKEN WITH PEPPERS AND ONIONS

*Although chicken typically looks a
bit pink after being steamed, it's thoroughly cooked
and safe to eat.*

¼ cup honey
2 teaspoons low-sodium soy sauce
¼ teaspoon salt
⅛ teaspoon pepper
4 cloves garlic, minced
4 (4-ounce) skinned, boned chicken breast
  halves
1 cup (2-inch) julienne-cut sweet red pepper
½ cup (1-inch) sliced green onions
2 tablespoons Spanish peanuts

Combine first 5 ingredients in a shallow dish; stir
well. Add chicken, sweet red pepper, and green
onions; turn to coat. Cover and marinate in refrigerator 1½ hours. Drain chicken and vegetables;
reserve marinade.

Arrange chicken in a foil-lined steamer over boiling water in a Dutch oven. Cover and steam 10
minutes. Add sweet red pepper and green onions.
Cover and steam an additional 6 minutes or until
chicken is done. Remove chicken and vegetables
from steamer; place on a serving platter.

Place marinade in a saucepan over medium heat;
bring marinade to a boil. Pour over chicken and
vegetables; top with peanuts. Yield: 4 servings.

PER SERVING: 231 CALORIES (15% FROM FAT)
FAT 3.8G (SATURATED FAT 0.7G)
PROTEIN 28.1G CARBOHYDRATE 21.6G
CHOLESTEROL 66MG SODIUM 290MG

CHICKEN BREASTS WITH MUSHROOM SAUCE

(pictured on cover)

1 (10½-ounce) can low-sodium chicken broth
2 tablespoons all-purpose flour
¼ teaspoon salt
¼ teaspoon pepper
4 (4-ounce) skinned, boned chicken breast
    halves
Vegetable cooking spray
1 tablespoon reduced-calorie margarine
2 cups sliced fresh mushrooms
2 tablespoons minced shallots
¼ cup dry sherry, divided
1½ teaspoons cornstarch
2 cups cooked long-grain rice
1 cup cooked wild rice
1 tablespoon chopped pecans
Citrus zest (optional)

Place broth in a small saucepan. Bring to a boil;
cook 5 minutes or until reduced to 1 cup. Set aside.

Combine flour, salt, and pepper; sprinkle over
chicken. Coat a large nonstick skillet with cooking
spray; place over medium-high heat until hot. Add
chicken; cook 5 minutes on each side or until
browned. Remove chicken from skillet, and set
aside. Wipe drippings from skillet.

Coat skillet with cooking spray; add margarine.
Place over medium-high heat until margarine
melts. Add mushrooms and shallots; sauté until
tender. Combine 1 tablespoon sherry and cornstarch; stir well, and set aside. Add remaining 3
tablespoons sherry and reduced broth to skillet.
Bring to a boil; cook until sauce is reduced to ¾
cup. Add cornstarch mixture; cook, stirring constantly, 1 minute or until mixture is thickened.

Return chicken to skillet; cover, reduce heat, and
simmer 10 minutes or until tender. Combine rices,
pecans, and citrus zest, if desired. Serve chicken
over rice mixture; top with mushroom sauce. Yield:
4 servings.

PER SERVING: 350 CALORIES (14% FROM FAT)
FAT 5.6G (SATURATED FAT 0.5G)
PROTEIN 32.1G   CARBOHYDRATE 41.7G
CHOLESTEROL 66MG   SODIUM 277MG

FRUITED CHICKEN WITH BOURBON AND PECANS

1 (16-ounce) can apricot halves in light syrup,
    undrained
3 tablespoons all-purpose flour
¼ teaspoon salt
⅛ teaspoon white pepper
6 (4-ounce) skinned, boned chicken breast
    halves
Vegetable cooking spray
2 teaspoons vegetable oil
1½ teaspoons cornstarch
3 tablespoons bourbon
1 teaspoon lemon juice
3 tablespoons chopped pecans, toasted
Fresh parsley sprigs (optional)

Drain apricots, reserving 1 cup syrup; set syrup
aside. Place 6 apricot halves, cut sides down, on a
cutting board. Reserve remaining apricots for other
uses. Cut slits in apricot halves to ¼ inch from one
end, forming a fan. Set aside.

Combine flour, salt, and pepper; dredge chicken
in flour mixture. Coat a large nonstick skillet with
cooking spray; add oil. Place over medium heat
until hot. Add chicken; cook 5 minutes on each
side or until done. Remove chicken from skillet;
transfer to a serving platter, and keep warm.

Combine reserved syrup, cornstarch, bourbon,
and lemon juice in a saucepan. Bring to a boil;
reduce heat, and simmer 2 minutes or until slightly
thickened, stirring constantly.

Place a fanned apricot half on each chicken
breast; top evenly with sauce. Sprinkle evenly with
pecans. Garnish with fresh parsley sprigs, if
desired. Yield: 6 servings.

PER SERVING: 233 CALORIES (22% FROM FAT)
FAT 5.7G (SATURATED FAT 0.9G)
PROTEIN 27.4G   CARBOHYDRATE 13.1G
CHOLESTEROL 66MG   SODIUM 173MG

Fruited Chicken with Bourbon and Pecans

RASPBERRY CHICKEN

When poaching the chicken, keep the liquid at a simmer. Boiling will overcook and toughen the outside of the chicken before the inside is fully cooked.

1   cup canned low-sodium chicken broth, undiluted
4   (4-ounce) skinned, boned chicken breast halves
¼   teaspoon pepper
¼   cup minced shallots
2   tablespoons raspberry vinegar
3   tablespoons low-sugar raspberry preserves
2   tablespoons low-fat sour cream
Fresh raspberries (optional)
Fresh mint sprigs (optional)

Place chicken broth in a large nonstick skillet. Bring to a boil; reduce heat, and simmer 5 minutes or until reduced to ½ cup.

Sprinkle chicken evenly with pepper. Add chicken, shallots, and vinegar to broth in skillet. Cover and simmer 20 minutes or until chicken is tender. Transfer to a serving platter, and keep warm.

Add preserves and sour cream to broth mixture, stirring with a wire whisk; cook, stirring constantly, until mixture is thoroughly heated. (Do not boil.) Spoon over chicken. If desired, garnish with fresh raspberries and mint sprigs. Yield: 4 servings.

PER SERVING: 154 CALORIES (16% FROM FAT)
FAT 2.7G (SATURATED FAT 1.0G)
PROTEIN 27.3G CARBOHYDRATE 5.3G
CHOLESTEROL 69MG SODIUM 99MG

SPINACH-STUFFED CHICKEN IN APRICOT SAUCE

1   (10-ounce) package frozen chopped spinach, thawed
½   cup 1% low-fat cottage cheese
⅓   cup fine, dry breadcrumbs
1   tablespoon minced shallot
¼   teaspoon salt
⅛   teaspoon garlic powder
⅛   teaspoon ground nutmeg
1   egg white
6   (4-ounce) skinned, boned chicken breast halves
1   tablespoon vegetable oil
1   cup apricot nectar
1   tablespoon tarragon vinegar
2   teaspoons brown sugar
2   teaspoons country-style Dijon mustard
6   medium-size unpeeled fresh apricots (about 12 ounces), each cut into 8 wedges

Press spinach between paper towels until barely moist. Combine spinach, cottage cheese, and next 6 ingredients in a bowl; stir well. Cut a horizontal slit through thickest portion of each breast half to form a pocket. Divide spinach mixture evenly among pockets. Cover chicken, and chill 1 hour.

Heat vegetable oil in a large nonstick skillet over medium heat until hot. Add chicken breast halves, and cook 7 minutes on each side or until done. Remove chicken breast halves from skillet; set aside, and keep warm.

Combine apricot nectar and next 3 ingredients in skillet; bring to a boil. Reduce heat, and simmer 7 minutes. Add apricot wedges, and simmer an additional 5 minutes or until sauce thickens. Serve sauce over chicken. Yield: 6 servings.

PER SERVING: 249 CALORIES (17% FROM FAT)
FAT 4.6G (SATURATED FAT 1.0G)
PROTEIN 32.0G CARBOHYDRATE 19.5G
CHOLESTEROL 67MG SODIUM 384MG

Spinach-Stuffed Chicken in Apricot Sauce

Breast of Chicken with Orange Sauce

6 (4-ounce) skinned, boned chicken breast
    halves
¼ teaspoon freshly ground pepper
1 tablespoon reduced-calorie margarine,
    melted
Vegetable cooking spray
1 tablespoon reduced-calorie margarine
1 tablespoon minced shallots
1 cup unsweetened orange juice
¼ cup Madeira
½ teaspoon minced garlic
1½ cups canned no-salt-added chicken broth,
    undiluted
¼ cup evaporated skimmed milk
⅛ teaspoon salt
⅛ teaspoon freshly ground pepper

Sprinkle chicken with ¼ teaspoon pepper, and brush with 1 tablespoon melted margarine. Place chicken on rack of a broiler pan coated with cooking spray. Bake at 375° for 16 to 18 minutes or until chicken is done. Transfer chicken to a serving platter, and keep warm.

Coat a small nonstick skillet with cooking spray; add 1 tablespoon margarine. Place over medium-high heat until margarine melts. Add shallots, and sauté 1 minute or until tender. Add orange juice, Madeira, and garlic; cook over high heat 14 minutes or until mixture is reduced to about ¼ cup. Add broth, and cook 15 minutes or until mixture is reduced to about ¾ cup.

Add evaporated skimmed milk to skillet, and cook 10 minutes or until mixture turns a caramel color and is reduced to about ¼ cup. Stir in salt and ⅛ teaspoon pepper. Drizzle sauce evenly over chicken breast halves. Yield: 6 servings.

PER SERVING: 198 CALORIES (25% FROM FAT)
FAT 5.6G (SATURATED FAT 1.2G)
PROTEIN 27.7G CARBOHYDRATE 7.1G
CHOLESTEROL 73MG SODIUM 164MG

Chicken Jambalaya
(pictured on page 102)

Round out this one-dish meal with a tossed salad, a wheat roll, and fresh fruit for dessert.

Vegetable cooking spray
1 teaspoon vegetable oil
¾ cup coarsely chopped lean cooked ham
    (about ¼ pound)
¾ cup chopped green pepper
½ cup chopped onion
½ cup chopped celery
2 cloves garlic, minced
2 cups canned low-sodium chicken broth,
    undiluted
1 (14½-ounce) can no-salt-added stewed
    tomatoes, undrained and chopped
1 cup chopped cooked chicken breast
⅔ cup long-grain rice, uncooked
1 bay leaf
1 teaspoon dried whole basil
½ teaspoon dried whole thyme
½ teaspoon chili powder
¼ teaspoon salt
¼ teaspoon pepper
½ teaspoon hot sauce

Coat a large skillet with cooking spray; add oil. Place over medium heat until hot. Add ham, green pepper, onion, celery, and garlic; sauté 5 minutes. Stir in chicken broth and remaining ingredients.

Bring broth mixture to a boil; cover, reduce heat, and simmer 15 minutes. Uncover and cook an additional 15 minutes or until rice is tender, stirring occasionally. Remove and discard bay leaf. Yield: 4 servings.

PER SERVING: 272 CALORIES (14% FROM FAT)
FAT 4.3G (SATURATED FAT 1.4G)
PROTEIN 19.6G CARBOHYDRATE 37.2G
CHOLESTEROL 44MG SODIUM 615MG

SWEET-AND-SOUR CHICKEN

1 (20-ounce) can unsweetened pineapple
  chunks, undrained
3 tablespoons white wine vinegar
3 tablespoons low-sodium soy sauce
3 tablespoons reduced-calorie catsup
1½ tablespoons cornstarch
1½ tablespoons brown sugar
2 teaspoons low-sodium Worcestershire sauce
½ teaspoon ground ginger
¼ teaspoon garlic powder
Vegetable cooking spray
¾ pound skinned, boned chicken breasts, cut
  into 1-inch cubes
½ small sweet red pepper, cut into julienne
  strips
½ small green pepper, cut into julienne strips
4 cups cooked long-grain rice (cooked without
  salt or fat)

Drain pineapple chunks, reserving juice. Set pineapple chunks aside. Combine reserved juice, vinegar, and next 7 ingredients in a small bowl; stir well, and set aside.

Coat a large nonstick skillet with cooking spray; place over medium-high heat until hot. Add chicken; cook 5 minutes or until chicken is browned on all sides. Add pineapple and pepper strips; cook 2 to 3 minutes or until pepper strips are crisp-tender, stirring constantly.

Gradually stir pineapple juice mixture into chicken mixture. Cook over medium heat, stirring constantly, until thickened and bubbly. Serve chicken mixture over rice. Yield: 4 servings.

PER SERVING: 443 CALORIES (3% FROM FAT)
FAT 1.5G (SATURATED FAT 0.3G)
PROTEIN 23.8G   CARBOHYDRATE 78.5G
CHOLESTEROL 49MG   SODIUM 364MG

SHERRIED CHICKEN AND BROCCOLI

1 tablespoon cornstarch
½ cup canned low-sodium chicken broth,
  undiluted
2 tablespoons low-sodium soy sauce
½ pound fresh broccoli
Vegetable cooking spray
2 teaspoons vegetable oil
½ pound skinned, boned chicken breasts, cut
  into bite-size pieces
1 clove garlic, minced
1 cup sliced carrot
1 medium onion, cut into 8 wedges
2 tablespoons dry sherry
4 cups cooked long-grain rice (cooked without
  salt or fat)

Combine first 3 ingredients; set aside. Trim leaves from broccoli, and remove tough ends of lower stalks. Cut flowerets into bite-size pieces and stalks into ¼-inch slices to yield 2 cups. Set aside.

Coat a large skillet with cooking spray; add oil, and place over medium-high heat until hot. Add chicken and garlic; sauté 3 minutes. Add carrot and onion; sauté 2 minutes. Add broccoli and sherry. Cover, reduce heat, and cook 4 minutes or until broccoli is crisp tender. Stir in cornstarch mixture. Cook 1 minute or until thickened, stirring constantly. Serve over rice. Yield: 4 servings.

PER SERVING: 364 CALORIES (9% FROM FAT)
FAT 3.7G (SATURATED FAT 0.7G)
PROTEIN 20.6G   CARBOHYDRATE 61.1G
CHOLESTEROL 33MG   SODIUM 311MG

FYI

Keeping oils in the refrigerator will lengthen their shelf life but may make some thicken or turn cloudy. Such oils are safe to use and usually become clear again at room temperature.

Chicken and Spinach Stir-Fry

CHICKEN AND SPINACH STIR-FRY

Vegetable cooking spray
2 teaspoons corn oil, divided
1 pound skinned, boned chicken breast halves,
    cut into thin strips
1 clove garlic, minced
½ pound sliced fresh mushrooms
1 cup canned low-sodium chicken broth,
    undiluted
¼ cup low-sodium soy sauce
1 tablespoon plus 1 teaspoon cornstarch
2 tablespoons Chablis or other dry white wine
1 teaspoon peeled, grated gingerroot
1 (8-ounce) can sliced water chestnuts,
    drained
2 cups sliced fresh spinach
4 cups cooked long-grain rice (cooked without
    salt or fat)

Coat a wok or large skillet with cooking spray.
Add 1 teaspoon oil around top of wok, coating
sides; heat at medium-high (375°) until hot. Add
chicken and garlic, and stir-fry 4 to 6 minutes or
until chicken is lightly browned. Remove chicken
from wok, and set aside. Wipe drippings from wok
with a paper towel.

Add 1 teaspoon oil around top of wok, and add
mushrooms to wok; stir fry 2 to 3 minutes or until
almost tender. Remove mushrooms from wok, and
set aside.

Combine broth, soy sauce, cornstarch, wine, and
gingerroot, stirring with a wire whisk until smooth.
Add chicken, broth mixture, and water chestnuts to
wok; bring to a boil, stirring constantly. Reduce
heat to low; cover and simmer 5 minutes. Stir in
mushrooms and spinach. Serve chicken mixture
over rice. Yield: 4 servings.

PER SERVING: 437 CALORIES (12% FROM FAT)
FAT 6.0G (SATURATED FAT 1.2G)
PROTEIN 33.2G CARBOHYDRATE 59.7G
CHOLESTEROL 72MG SODIUM 566MG

*Stir-fry thin strips of chicken in a
wok coated with cooking spray and
only a small amount of oil. Stir constantly to cook chicken evenly.*

*Stop cooking the mushrooms before
they are completely tender for a crisp
texture.*

*After adding the mushrooms and
spinach, cook just until heated so the
spinach will not overcook.*

COUNTRY CAPTAIN STIR-FRY

Vegetable cooking spray
2 teaspoons vegetable oil, divided
1 pound skinned, boned chicken breasts, cut into ½-inch-wide strips
1 medium-size sweet onion, thinly sliced
1 clove garlic, minced
1½ teaspoons curry powder
½ teaspoon salt
½ teaspoon dried whole thyme, crushed
⅛ teaspoon ground red pepper
⅛ teaspoon sugar
1 large green pepper, cut into thin strips
1 large sweet red pepper, cut into thin strips
1 pound tomatoes, peeled, seeded, and cut into wedges
½ cup canned low-sodium chicken broth, undiluted
¼ cup raisins
3 cups cooked long-grain rice (cooked without salt or fat)
2 tablespoons slivered almonds, toasted
2 tablespoons chopped fresh parsley

Coat a wok or skillet with cooking spray; add 1 teaspoon vegetable oil. Heat at medium-high (375°) until hot. Add chicken; stir-fry 3 minutes. Remove chicken from wok, and drain on paper towels. Wipe drippings from wok with a paper towel.

Add remaining 1 teaspoon vegetable oil to wok; place over medium-high heat until hot. Add onion and garlic; stir-fry 3 minutes or until tender. Add curry powder and next 4 ingredients; stir well. Add pepper strips, and stir-fry 1 minute. Add tomato, chicken broth, and raisins, stirring well; bring tomato mixture to a boil. Stir-fry mixture 3 minutes or until liquid is reduced by half.

Return chicken to wok. Cook, stirring constantly, until thoroughly heated. Spoon chicken mixture over cooked rice, and sprinkle with almonds and parsley. Yield: 6 servings.

PER SERVING: 281 CALORIES (17% FROM FAT)
FAT 5.2G (SATURATED FAT 1.0G)
PROTEIN 21.0G CARBOHYDRATE 37.2G
CHOLESTEROL 47MG SODIUM 245MG

CHICKEN-ASPARAGUS STIR-FRY

1½ pounds skinned, boned chicken breasts
¼ cup water
2 tablespoons low-sodium soy sauce
2 tablespoons dry sherry
¼ teaspoon garlic powder
¼ teaspoon chicken-flavored bouillon granules
¼ teaspoon ground ginger
2 teaspoons cornstarch
Vegetable cooking spray
1 pound fresh asparagus spears, cut into 1-inch pieces
1 medium onion, thinly sliced
½ pound fresh mushrooms, sliced
2 medium tomatoes, unpeeled and cut into wedges
3 cups cooked long-grain rice (cooked without salt or fat)

Cut chicken into ¼-inch strips, and place in a shallow container. Combine water and next 5 ingredients; stir well. Pour mixture over chicken; cover and refrigerate 30 minutes. Drain chicken, reserving marinade. Combine marinade and cornstarch, stirring until smooth. Set aside.

Coat a nonstick wok or large skillet with cooking spray; heat at medium-high (375°) for 2 minutes. Add chicken to wok; stir-fry 3 to 4 minutes. Remove chicken from wok, and drain on paper towels; set aside. Wipe drippings from wok with a paper towel.

Coat wok with cooking spray. Add asparagus and onion to wok; stir-fry at medium-high heat 3 minutes. Add mushrooms; stir-fry 2 minutes. Return chicken to wok. Pour reserved marinade mixture over chicken and vegetables, stirring well. Add tomato; cook 2 to 3 minutes or until sauce thickens. Serve over rice. Yield: 6 servings.

PER SERVING: 304 CALORIES (11% FROM FAT)
FAT 3.8G (SATURATED FAT 1.0G)
PROTEIN 30.6G CARBOHYDRATE 35.1G
CHOLESTEROL 68MG SODIUM 266MG

CHICKEN STIR-FRY CALCUTTA

1 (10½-ounce) can low-sodium chicken broth
2 tablespoons cornstarch
1 tablespoon peeled, grated gingerroot
2 teaspoons low-sodium soy sauce
½ teaspoon coriander seed
½ teaspoon ground cumin
¼ teaspoon salt
¼ teaspoon ground cardamom
¼ teaspoon pepper
¾ pound fresh snow pea pods
Vegetable cooking spray
2 teaspoons vegetable oil, divided
4 (4-ounce) skinned, boned chicken breast halves, cut into thin strips
1 medium-size sweet red pepper, cut into thin strips
5 green onions, cut into 1-inch pieces
1 cup sliced celery
3 cups cooked long-grain rice (cooked without salt or fat)
2 tablespoons chopped unsalted peanuts

Combine first 9 ingredients; stir well. Set aside. Wash snow peas; trim ends, and remove strings. Set aside.

Coat a wok or large nonstick skillet with cooking spray; add 1 teaspoon oil. Heat at medium-high (375°) until hot. Add chicken, and stir-fry 3 minutes or until lightly browned. Remove chicken from wok, and drain on paper towels. Wipe drippings from wok with a paper towel.

Add remaining 1 teaspoon oil to wok; heat at medium-high until hot. Add snow peas, sweet red pepper, green onions, and celery; stir-fry 3 to 4 minutes or until vegetables are crisp-tender. Add reserved chicken broth mixture; stir well.

Return chicken to wok. Cook, stirring constantly, until mixture is thickened and thoroughly heated. Serve over rice; sprinkle with chopped peanuts. Yield: 6 servings.

PER SERVING: 291 CALORIES (19% FROM FAT)
FAT 6.3G (SATURATED FAT 1.2G)
PROTEIN 22.7G   CARBOHYDRATE 34.2G
CHOLESTEROL 47MG   SODIUM 207MG

CHICKEN FRIED RICE

This variation of an Oriental favorite is hearty enough to serve as the main course for a casual supper. Offer a fresh fruit salad and hot bread on the side.

3 (4-ounce) skinned, boned chicken breast halves
2 cups water
2 tablespoons reduced-sodium soy sauce
1 egg, lightly beaten
½ teaspoon pepper
Vegetable cooking spray
2 teaspoons peanut oil
½ cup finely chopped fresh mushrooms
¼ cup thinly sliced green onions
2 cups cooked long-grain rice (cooked without salt or fat)

Combine chicken and water in a large saucepan. Bring to a boil; cover, reduce heat, and simmer 15 to 20 minutes or until chicken is tender. Remove chicken, reserving broth. Cut chicken into ¾-inch pieces, and set aside.

Skim and discard fat from broth, reserving ⅓ cup broth; save remaining broth for other uses.

Combine reserved ⅓ cup broth, soy sauce, egg, and pepper; stir well. Set aside.

Coat a wok or large nonstick skillet with cooking spray; add oil. Heat at medium-high (375°) until hot. Add mushrooms and green onions; stir-fry 3 minutes. Stir in rice and chicken. Cook, stirring frequently, 6 to 8 minutes or until thoroughly heated. Drizzle egg mixture over rice and chicken mixture, stirring constantly, until egg is soft-cooked. Serve warm. Yield: 4 servings.

PER SERVING: 263 CALORIES (21% FROM FAT)
FAT 6.2G (SATURATED FAT 1.4G)
PROTEIN 23.8G   CARBOHYDRATE 26.0G
CHOLESTEROL 108MG   SODIUM 317MG

Oriental Chicken Stir-Fry

ORIENTAL CHICKEN STIR-FRY

1 pound skinned, boned chicken breasts, cut into 1-inch cubes
⅓ cup Chablis or other dry white wine
⅓ cup teriyaki sauce
2 teaspoons peeled, grated gingerroot
1 clove garlic, crushed
1 cup canned no-salt-added chicken broth, undiluted
1½ tablespoons low-sodium soy sauce
1 tablespoon cornstarch
1½ teaspoons brown sugar
Vegetable cooking spray
1 tablespoon sesame oil, divided
3 cups fresh broccoli flowerets
2 medium-size sweet red peppers, cut into julienne strips
½ cup chopped green onions
5 cups cooked long-grain rice (cooked without salt or fat)

Place chicken in a heavy-duty, zip-top plastic bag. Combine wine, teriyaki sauce, gingerroot, and garlic in a small bowl, stirring well. Pour over chicken; seal bag, and shake until chicken is well coated. Marinate in refrigerator 2 to 4 hours, turning bag occasionally.

Remove chicken from marinade; discard marinade. Combine broth, soy sauce, cornstarch, and brown sugar; stir well, and set aside.

Coat a wok or large nonstick skillet with vegetable cooking spray; add 2 teaspoons oil. Heat at medium-high (375°) until hot. Add chicken, and stir-fry 4 to 5 minutes or until tender. Remove chicken from wok, and drain on paper towels; set aside. Wipe drippings from wok with a paper towel.

Add remaining 1 teaspoon oil to wok; heat at medium-high until hot. Add broccoli, and stir-fry 2 minutes. Add pepper strips and green onions; stir-fry 3 to 4 minutes or until crisp-tender. Remove vegetables from wok, and set aside.

Add broth mixture to wok; cook, stirring constantly, until mixture is thickened. Return chicken and vegetables to wok; cook, stirring constantly, until mixture is thoroughly heated. Serve chicken mixture over rice. Yield: 5 servings.

PER SERVING: 412 CALORIES (14% FROM FAT)
FAT 6.3G (SATURATED FAT 1.3G)
PROTEIN 28.7G CARBOHYDRATE 57.5G
CHOLESTEROL 60MG SODIUM 488MG

CHICKEN WITH CRUNCHY VEGETABLES

¾ pound skinned, boned chicken breasts, cut into 1-inch pieces
¼ cup low-sodium teriyaki sauce, divided
Vegetable cooking spray
1 teaspoon dark sesame oil
1 cup diagonally sliced celery
¾ cup thinly sliced carrot
1 clove garlic, crushed
1 cup coarsely shredded red cabbage
1 (8-ounce) can sliced water chestnuts, drained

Combine chicken and 1 tablespoon teriyaki sauce in a bowl; stir well. Let stand 10 minutes.

Coat a wok or large nonstick skillet with cooking spray; drizzle oil around top of wok, coating sides. Heat at medium-high (375°) until hot. Add celery, carrot, and garlic; stir-fry 1 minute. Remove celery mixture from wok.

Add chicken to wok, and stir-fry 3 minutes. Add remaining 3 tablespoons teriyaki sauce, and stir-fry 1 minute. Add celery mixture, red cabbage, and water chestnuts to wok; stir-fry 1 minute or until chicken is done and cabbage is crisp-tender. Yield: 4 servings.

PER SERVING: 161 CALORIES (14% FROM FAT)
FAT 2.5G (SATURATED FAT 0.5G)
PROTEIN 21.7G CARBOHYDRATE 11.9G
CHOLESTEROL 49MG SODIUM 395MG

FIRE UP THE GRILL

*A*nyone who heats up the coals and throws chicken on the grill vies for instant popularity. The appetizing aroma is sure to tempt even the shyest neighbors. Go ahead—invite them over. Grilling is easy and a marvelous way to entertain a crowd. Depending on the number of guests, split a broiler-fryer in half or choose a package of favorite pieces: legs, thighs, drumsticks, or breast halves. In addition, try one of the sauces or marinades to enhance the flavor and keep the chicken from drying out.

Give this collection of recipes a try. You'll discover that few people can resist the call of the grill. And they'll never guess how light these entrées are.

Dijon-Glazed Chicken (Recipe follows on page 134)

ZESTY BARBECUED CHICKEN

1 (3½-pound) broiler-fryer, cut up and skinned
1 (8-ounce) can tomato sauce
½ teaspoon grated lemon rind
¼ cup lemon juice
1 tablespoon brown sugar
2 tablespoons vinegar
1 tablespoon Worcestershire sauce
1 teaspoon prepared mustard
¼ teaspoon ground red pepper
¼ teaspoon black pepper
1 clove garlic, crushed

Place chicken in a 12- x 8- x 2-inch baking dish, and set aside.

Combine remaining ingredients in a small saucepan. Bring to a boil. Cover; reduce heat, and simmer 20 minutes. Pour sauce over chicken. Cover and marinate in refrigerator 8 hours, turning chicken occasionally.

Remove chicken from sauce, reserving sauce. Place chicken, bone side down, on grill rack over medium coals. Grill 45 minutes to 1 hour or until chicken is done, turning and basting with sauce every 15 minutes. Yield: 6 servings.

PER SERVING: 314 CALORIES (32% FROM FAT)
FAT 11.3G (SATURATED FAT 3.1G)
PROTEIN 44.4G   CARBOHYDRATE 6.9G
CHOLESTEROL 135MG   SODIUM 395MG

BARBECUED CHICKEN

½ cup finely chopped onion
¼ cup firmly packed brown sugar
2 tablespoons cider vinegar
2 tablespoons prepared mustard
1½ teaspoons chili powder
1 teaspoon Worcestershire sauce
1 large clove garlic, minced
1 (13¼-ounce) bottle reduced-calorie catsup
Vegetable cooking spray
8 (6-ounce) skinned chicken breast halves

Combine first 8 ingredients in a saucepan; stir well. Bring to a boil over medium heat. Cover, reduce heat, and simmer 20 minutes.

Coat grill rack with cooking spray; place on grill over medium-hot coals. Place chicken, bone side up, on rack; grill 10 minutes. Turn chicken over; baste with catsup mixture. Grill an additional 30 to 40 minutes or until chicken is done, turning and basting every 5 minutes. Yield: 8 servings.

PER SERVING: 220 CALORIES (16% FROM FAT)
FAT 3.9G (SATURATED FAT 1.0G)
PROTEIN 31.2G   CARBOHYDRATE 11.9G
CHOLESTEROL 84MG   SODIUM 146MG

Grilling Hints

Here are some suggestions for successful grilling of chicken.

• Shorten grilling time for chicken and other meat by partially cooking it in the microwave oven before grilling.

• Coat the grill rack with vegetable cooking spray before grilling to prevent sticking. Arrange the rack 6 to 8 inches above the coals.

• The key to good grilled chicken is the proper temperature of the fire and adequate cooking time. For most recipes, coals should be covered with a light gray ash before placing chicken on the grill rack.

• Chicken legs, drumsticks, and thighs require longer grilling time than chicken breasts.

• Place grilled chicken on a clean platter, not on the dish used to hold raw chicken, unless the dish has been washed thoroughly.

Barbecued Chicken

Thai Chicken Barbecue

¼ cup firmly packed brown sugar
¼ cup low-sodium soy sauce
1 tablespoon fresh lime juice
3 cloves garlic, minced
½ teaspoon crushed red pepper
¼ to ½ teaspoon curry powder
1 (3-pound) broiler-fryer, cut up and skinned
Vegetable cooking spray
Green onion fans (optional)

Combine first 6 ingredients in an extra-large heavy-duty, zip-top plastic bag; add chicken. Seal bag, and marinate in refrigerator at least 4 hours, turning occasionally.

Remove chicken from marinade, reserving marinade. Transfer marinade to a small saucepan; bring to a boil. Reduce heat, and simmer 3 minutes.

Coat grill rack with cooking spray; place on grill over medium-hot coals. Place chicken on rack, and grill 20 to 25 minutes or until chicken is done, turning and basting frequently with marinade. Transfer to a large serving platter. Garnish with green onion fans, if desired. Yield: 6 servings.

Per Serving: 197 Calories (28% from fat)
Fat 6.1g (Saturated Fat 1.7g)
Protein 23.7g   Carbohydrate 9.7g
Cholesterol 73mg   Sodium 333mg

Grilled Herbed Chicken

½ teaspoon dried whole basil
½ teaspoon dried whole thyme
½ teaspoon dried whole oregano
6 (4-ounce) skinned, boned chicken breast halves
1 tablespoon olive oil
3 tablespoons lemon juice
Vegetable cooking spray

Combine basil, thyme, and oregano in a small bowl; set aside.

Place chicken between 2 sheets of heavy-duty plastic wrap; flatten to ¼-inch thickness, using a meat mallet or rolling pin. Brush chicken with olive oil; sprinkle with lemon juice and herb mixture.

Coat grill rack with cooking spray. Place rack on grill 6 inches above medium coals. Place chicken on rack. Grill 10 minutes or until chicken is tender, turning once. Yield: 6 servings.

Per Serving: 164 Calories (30% from fat)
Fat 5.4g (Saturated Fat 1.2g)
Protein 26.4g   Carbohydrate 0.9g
Cholesterol 72mg   Sodium 63mg

Marinades

Marinating chicken adds flavor and also helps to keep the chicken moist. It's especially recommended for skinned, boned chicken breasts, which cook very quickly and tend to dry out on the grill.

• Marinate chicken in the refrigerator, not on the kitchen counter at room temperature.

• Marinades should not be served as a sauce for cooked chicken unless the marinade is first heated to a boil to kill any bacteria.

• Commercial low-fat or fat-free marinades are available, or you can make your own with low-fat ingredients such as citrus juices, wines, and flavored vinegars.

Marinate chicken in a zip-top plastic bag in the refrigerator, turning the bag occasionally.

Hawaiian Chicken

HAWAIIAN CHICKEN

¼ cup unsweetened orange juice
2 tablespoons unsweetened pineapple juice
1 teaspoon minced fresh cilantro
¼ teaspoon salt
4 (6-ounce) skinned chicken breast halves
¾ cup finely chopped fresh pineapple
1 tablespoon plus 1 teaspoon finely chopped
     sweet red pepper
1 teaspoon finely chopped jalapeño pepper
1½ teaspoons minced fresh cilantro
1½ teaspoons white wine vinegar
1 teaspoon unsweetened orange juice
½ teaspoon pepper
Vegetable cooking spray
Fresh pineapple leaves (optional)

Combine first 4 ingredients in a shallow dish; mix well. Add chicken, turning to coat well. Cover and marinate chicken in refrigerator 6 to 8 hours, turning occasionally.

Combine pineapple and next 5 ingredients in a small bowl; mix well. Let mixture stand at room temperature 2 hours.

Remove chicken from dish, reserving marinade. Sprinkle chicken with ½ teaspoon pepper.

Coat grill rack with cooking spray; place on grill 4 to 5 inches above medium-hot coals. Place chicken on rack, and grill 15 minutes or until done, turning and basting frequently with reserved marinade.

To serve, top chicken breast half with about 3 tablespoons pineapple mixture. Garnish with pineapple leaves, if desired. Yield: 4 servings.

PER SERVING: 170 CALORIES (17% FROM FAT)
FAT 3.3G (SATURATED FAT 0.8G)
PROTEIN 26.7G   CARBOHYDRATE 7.0G
CHOLESTEROL 72MG   SODIUM 211MG

LIME CHICKEN WITH BLACK BEAN SAUCE

3 tablespoons fresh lime juice
1½ tablespoons vegetable oil
¼ teaspoon ground red pepper
4 cloves garlic, crushed
4 (4-ounce) skinned, boned chicken breast
   halves
Vegetable cooking spray
2 cups water
½ cup diced sweet red pepper
1 tablespoon chopped purple onion
1 cup drained canned black beans
½ cup unsweetened orange juice
2 tablespoons balsamic vinegar
¼ teaspoon salt
⅛ teaspoon freshly ground black pepper
2 cloves garlic, crushed
Fresh cilantro sprigs (optional)

Combine first 4 ingredients in a large heavy-duty, zip-top plastic bag. Add chicken; seal bag, and marinate in refrigerator 8 hours, turning occasionally.

Remove chicken from bag, reserving marinade. Coat grill rack with cooking spray; place on grill over medium-hot coals. Place chicken on rack, and grill 7 minutes on each side or until chicken is done, basting occasionally with reserved marinade. Set chicken aside, and keep warm.

Bring water to a boil in a small saucepan; add sweet red pepper and onion. Cook 30 seconds; drain. Plunge into ice water; drain well. Set aside.

Position knife blade in food processor bowl; add beans and next 5 ingredients. Process until smooth. Cook in saucepan over medium heat until heated.

Spoon ¼ cup plus 1 tablespoon bean mixture onto each of 4 serving plates. Place chicken breast halves on top of sauce; top each with 2 tablespoons sweet red pepper mixture. Garnish with fresh cilantro, if desired. Yield: 4 servings.

PER SERVING: 292 CALORIES (27% FROM FAT)
FAT 8.9G (SATURATED FAT 1.9G)
PROTEIN 32.2.7G CARBOHYDRATE 20.9G
CHOLESTEROL 72MG SODIUM 305MG

CHICKEN AND VEGETABLE PACKETS

1 teaspoon salt-free lemon-pepper seasoning
½ teaspoon onion powder
½ teaspoon garlic powder
¼ teaspoon dried whole thyme
1 small sweet red pepper, sliced
1 medium zucchini, sliced
1 medium carrot, scraped and sliced
Vegetable cooking spray
4 (4-ounce) skinned, boned chicken breast
   halves
½ cup Chablis or other dry white wine

Combine first 4 ingredients in a small bowl, and stir well.

Combine sweet red pepper, zucchini, and carrot slices in a medium bowl. Add 1¼ teaspoons seasoning mixture to vegetable mixture, and toss gently to coat.

Cut 4 (18- x 12-inch) pieces of heavy-duty aluminum foil; coat foil with cooking spray. Place 1 chicken breast half on one end of each piece of foil; sprinkle chicken evenly with remaining 1 teaspoon seasoning mixture. Spoon one-fourth of vegetable mixture over each chicken breast half; sprinkle 2 tablespoons wine over each. For each packet, fold end of foil over chicken, bringing edges together. Fold edges over to seal; pleat and crimp edges of foil to make an airtight seal.

Place grill rack over medium coals. Place chicken packets on rack, and grill 15 minutes or until packets are puffed and chicken is done. Remove packets from grill. Cut an opening in the top of each packet, and fold foil back. Spoon chicken and vegetables onto individual serving plates, and top with remaining juices. Yield: 4 servings.

PER SERVING: 159 CALORIES (12% FROM FAT)
FAT 2.1G (SATURATED FAT 0.4G)
PROTEIN 27.5G CARBOHYDRATE 6.8G
CHOLESTEROL 66MG SODIUM 88MG

Chicken and Vegetable Packets

DIJON-GLAZED CHICKEN
(pictured on page 126)

Skinned, boned chicken breast halves can be grilled in about 10 minutes. For a different cooking method, follow the baking instructions, and prepare the rest of the meal while the chicken is in the oven.

2 tablespoons Dijon mustard
1 tablespoon brown sugar
1 tablespoon honey
1 teaspoon peeled, minced gingerroot
Vegetable cooking spray
4 (4-ounce) skinned, boned chicken breast
   halves
Fresh parsley sprigs (optional)

Combine mustard, sugar, honey, and gingerroot in a small bowl; stir well.

Coat grill rack with cooking spray; place on grill over medium-hot coals. Place chicken on rack, brushing half of mustard mixture over chicken. Grill 5 minutes; turn chicken, and brush with remaining mustard mixture. Grill an additional 5 minutes or until chicken is done. Transfer chicken to a serving platter. Garnish with fresh parsley sprigs, if desired. Yield: 4 servings.

PER SERVING: 160 CALORIES (12% FROM FAT)
FAT 2.1G (SATURATED FAT 0.4G)
PROTEIN 26.2G CARBOHYDRATE 7.1G
CHOLESTEROL 66MG SODIUM 298MG

Baking Instructions: Place chicken in an 11- x 7- x 2-inch baking dish coated with cooking spray. Brush mustard mixture over chicken. Cover and bake at 375° for 15 to 20 minutes or until chicken is done. Uncover and broil chicken 4 inches from heat (with electric oven door partially opened) 1 to 2 minutes or until golden.

HONEY CHICKEN WITH CHERRY SAUCE

⅓ cup Burgundy or other dry red wine
3 tablespoons brown sugar
2 tablespoons red wine vinegar
2 tablespoons unsweetened orange juice
¼ teaspoon grated orange rind
2¼ cups pitted quartered sweet cherries
   (about 1 pound)
2 teaspoons cornstarch
2 teaspoons water
2 tablespoons honey
2 tablespoons lemon juice
6 chicken leg quarters, skinned
½ teaspoon salt
¼ teaspoon pepper
Vegetable cooking spray

Combine first 5 ingredients in a medium saucepan; stir well. Bring to a boil over medium heat, and cook 5 minutes. Reduce heat to medium-low; add cherries, and cook 10 minutes, stirring occasionally.

Combine cornstarch and water; stir well, and add to cherry mixture. Bring to a boil over medium heat, and cook 1 minute or until slightly thickened, stirring constantly. Pour into a bowl; set aside, and keep warm.

Combine honey and lemon juice; stir well, and set aside.

Sprinkle chicken with salt and pepper. Coat grill rack with cooking spray, and place on grill over medium-hot coals. Place chicken on rack, and grill 25 minutes, turning every 5 minutes. Lightly brush chicken with half of honey mixture; grill 5 minutes. Turn chicken; brush with remaining honey mixture. Grill 5 minutes or until chicken is done. Serve each leg quarter with ¼ cup cherry sauce. Yield: 6 servings.

PER SERVING: 257 CALORIES (30% FROM FAT)
FAT 8.7G (SATURATED FAT 2.3G)
PROTEIN 23.4G CARBOHYDRATE 21.5G
CHOLESTEROL 77MG SODIUM 276MG

Honey Chicken with Cherry Sauce

Cold Grilled Chicken with Exotic Fruit

COLD GRILLED CHICKEN WITH EXOTIC FRUIT

8 (4-ounce) skinned, boned chicken breast
    halves
¾ cup unsweetened pineapple juice
¼ cup reduced-sodium soy sauce
2 tablespoons lime juice
1 clove garlic, minced
8 mesquite chips
Vegetable cooking spray
Blueberry Sauce
1 medium star fruit, cut into 8 slices
2 medium kiwifruit, peeled and cut into
    8 slices each
8 medium-size fresh strawberries

Place chicken in a shallow container. Combine
pineapple juice, soy sauce, lime juice, and garlic,
stirring well. Pour over chicken; cover and marinate
in refrigerator 8 hours, turning occasionally. Drain;
reserve marinade.

Cover mesquite chips with water, and soak 30
minutes. Drain chips, and place directly on medium coals. Coat grill rack with cooking spray; place
on grill 4 to 5 inches above medium-hot coals.
Place chicken on rack, and grill 5 minutes on each
side or until chicken is tender, basting once with
reserved marinade. Remove chicken from grill, and
chill thoroughly.

Spoon 2 tablespoons Blueberry Sauce onto each
of 8 serving plates. Place chicken breast halves in
Blueberry Sauce. Top each serving with 1 slice of
star fruit, 2 slices of kiwifruit, and 1 strawberry.
Yield: 8 servings.

BLUEBERRY SAUCE
1 cup fresh blueberries
2 tablespoons water
2 tablespoons crème de cassis
1 teaspoon lemon juice

Combine blueberries, water, and crème de cassis
in a small saucepan. Bring to a boil; reduce heat,
and simmer 1 to 2 minutes. Remove from heat and
cool. Transfer mixture to container of an electric
blender or food processor; cover and process until
smooth. Stir in lemon juice. Cover and chill thoroughly. Yield: 1 cup.

PER SERVING: 195 CALORIES (16% FROM FAT)
FAT 3.4G (SATURATED FAT 0.9G)
PROTEIN 27.4G CARBOHYDRATE 11.6G
CHOLESTEROL 72MG SODIUM 307MG

PINEAPPLE-GRILLED CHICKEN

1 (8-ounce) can unsweetened pineapple slices,
    undrained
½ cup unsweetened apple juice
1 tablespoon honey
1 teaspoon chicken-flavored bouillon granules
2 tablespoons raisins
Vegetable cooking spray
4 (4-ounce) skinned, boned chicken breast
    halves

Drain pineapple, reserving juice; set pineapple
slices aside.

Combine pineapple juice, apple juice, honey,
and bouillon granules in a small nonaluminum
saucepan. Bring mixture to a boil. Add raisins.
Cover, reduce heat, and simmer 5 minutes.
Remove raisins with a slotted spoon; set raisins and
juice mixture aside.

Coat grill rack with cooking spray; place on grill
over medium-hot coals. Place pineapple slices on
rack; grill 3 minutes on each side. Set aside. Place
chicken on rack; grill 15 minutes or until chicken is
tender, turning and basting frequently with
reserved juice mixture.

Place chicken on a serving platter. Top each
breast half with a grilled pineapple slice. Spoon any
remaining juice mixture over pineapple. Sprinkle
raisins evenly over pineapple. Yield: 4 servings.

PER SERVING: 221 CALORIES (15% FROM FAT)
FAT 3.6G (SATURATED FAT 1.0G)
PROTEIN 26.0G CARBOHYDRATE 20.7G
CHOLESTEROL 70MG SODIUM 273MG

GRILLED CHICKEN WITH RASPBERRY-THYME SAUCE

1 cup fresh raspberries
2½ tablespoons minced fresh thyme
1 teaspoon sugar
2 tablespoons Chablis or other dry white wine
1½ teaspoons low-sodium soy sauce
4 (4-ounce) skinned, boned chicken breast
    halves
½ teaspoon white pepper
Vegetable cooking spray
Fresh thyme sprigs (optional)

Place raspberries in a small bowl and crush. Add minced fresh thyme and next 3 ingredients, stirring well; let stand 30 minutes. Strain raspberry mixture; discard solids.

Place raspberry mixture in a small nonaluminum saucepan, and cook over medium heat 7 minutes or until thickened, stirring frequently. Remove from heat, and set aside.

Sprinkle chicken with pepper. Coat grill rack with cooking spray, and place on grill over medium-hot coals. Place chicken on rack, and grill 10 minutes. Turn chicken; brush with 2 tablespoons raspberry mixture, and grill an additional 5 minutes or until done.

Spoon 1 tablespoon remaining raspberry mixture over each chicken breast half to serve. Garnish with thyme sprigs, if desired. Yield: 4 servings.

PER SERVING: 175 CALORIES (22% FROM FAT)
FAT 4.2G (SATURATED FAT 1.1G)
PROTEIN 26.6G   CARBOHYDRATE 5.2G
CHOLESTEROL 72MG   SODIUM 127MG

SANTA FE-STYLE GRILLED CHICKEN BREASTS

4 (4-ounce) skinned, boned chicken breast
    halves
¼ teaspoon salt
¼ teaspoon pepper
⅓ cup lime juice
2 teaspoons olive oil
1¾ cups diced plum tomato (about ¾ pound)
⅓ cup chopped onion
3 tablespoons minced fresh cilantro
2 tablespoons red wine vinegar
1 tablespoon seeded, minced jalapeño pepper
Vegetable cooking spray

Place chicken between 2 sheets of heavy-duty plastic wrap, and flatten to ½-inch thickness, using a meat mallet or rolling pin. Make ⅛-inch-deep diagonal slits in each chicken breast, forming a diamond pattern. Sprinkle chicken with salt and pepper; place in a shallow dish.

Combine lime juice and olive oil in a bowl; stir well, and pour over chicken. Cover chicken, and marinate in refrigerator 3 hours, turning occasionally.

Combine tomato and next 4 ingredients in a small bowl; stir well. Cover and chill thoroughly.

Remove chicken from marinade, discarding marinade. Coat grill rack with cooking spray; place on grill over medium-hot coals. Place chicken on rack, and grill 5 to 6 minutes on each side or until done. Cut chicken into thin slices. Serve with chilled tomato mixture. Yield: 4 servings.

PER SERVING: 171 CALORIES (21% FROM FAT)
FAT 4.0G (SATURATED FAT 1.0G)
PROTEIN 26.7G   CARBOHYDRATE 6.2G
CHOLESTEROL 70MG   SODIUM 218MG

CHICKEN WITH DILL SAUCE

8 (4-ounce) skinned, boned chicken breast halves
½ cup commercial reduced-calorie Italian dressing
2 tablespoons water
1 tablespoon lime juice
1 tablespoon white wine vinegar
1 clove garlic, crushed
Vegetable cooking spray
Lime wedges
Dill Sauce

Place chicken between 2 sheets of heavy-duty plastic wrap; flatten to ¼-inch thickness, using a meat mallet or rolling pin. Place chicken in a 13- x 9- x 2-inch baking dish. Combine Italian dressing and next 4 ingredients in a small bowl; pour over chicken. Cover and marinate in refrigerator 2 hours.

Remove chicken from marinade, discarding marinade. Coat grill rack with cooking spray. Place chicken on rack, and grill 6 inches above medium coals 5 minutes on each side or until done.

Arrange chicken on a serving platter; garnish with lime wedges. Serve warm or chilled with 1½ tablespoons Dill Sauce per serving. Yield: 8 servings.

DILL SAUCE

½ cup plain low-fat yogurt
¼ cup low-fat cottage cheese
1½ teaspoons lime juice
1½ teaspoons chopped green onion
½ teaspoon dried whole dillweed
⅛ teaspoon white pepper

Combine all ingredients in container of an electric blender; cover and process until smooth. Cover and chill thoroughly. Yield: ¾ cup.

PER SERVING: 157 CALORIES (19% FROM FAT)
FAT 3.4G (SATURATED FAT 1.1G)
PROTEIN 28.0G   CARBOHYDRATE 1.5G
CHOLESTEROL 73MG   SODIUM 129MG

BUFFALO CHICKEN

4 (4-ounce) skinned, boned chicken breast halves
¼ cup light beer
¼ cup hot sauce
2 tablespoons white wine vinegar
¼ teaspoon cracked pepper
Vegetable cooking spray
¼ cup commercial nonfat blue cheese dressing

Place chicken between 2 sheets of heavy-duty plastic wrap, and flatten to ¼-inch thickness, using a meat mallet or rolling pin. Place chicken in a heavy-duty, zip-top plastic bag. Combine beer, hot sauce, vinegar, and pepper; pour over chicken. Seal bag; marinate in refrigerator 10 minutes.

Drain chicken, discarding marinade. Coat grill rack with cooking spray; place on grill over medium-hot coals. Place chicken on rack, and grill 5 minutes on each side or until done. Serve with blue cheese dressing. Yield: 4 servings.

PER SERVING: 160 CALORIES (19% FROM FAT)
FAT 3.3G (SATURATED FAT 0.9G)
PROTEIN 27.6G   CARBOHYDRATE 2.4G
CHOLESTEROL 75MG   SODIUM 258MG

Grilling Hints

You can judge the temperature of coals in the grill by placing an oven thermometer on the grill rack.

When the recipe calls for:	Thermometer should read:
low coals	under 300°
medium coals	300° to 350°
medium-hot coals	350° to 400°
hot coals	400° to 500°

CHICKEN SATÉ KABOBS

¾ cup chopped onion
1 tablespoon brown sugar
1 tablespoon creamy peanut butter
2 tablespoons lemon juice
1 tablespoon low-sodium soy sauce
2 cloves garlic, peeled
¼ teaspoon hot sauce
4 (4-ounce) skinned, boned chicken breast
　　halves, cut into ½-inch-wide strips
1 medium-size sweet red pepper, cut into
　　1-inch pieces
Vegetable cooking spray
2 cups cooked long-grain rice (cooked without
　　salt or fat)

Combine first 7 ingredients in container of an electric blender; cover and process until smooth, scraping sides of container occasionally.

Place chicken in a heavy-duty, zip-top plastic bag; add onion mixture. Seal and marinate in refrigerator 15 minutes, turning once.

Drain chicken, and discard marinade. Thread chicken and pepper pieces alternately on 8 (10-inch) skewers.

Coat grill rack with cooking spray; place on grill over medium-hot coals. Place chicken kabobs on rack, and grill 10 to 12 minutes or until chicken is done, turning occasionally. Serve kabobs over rice. Yield: 4 servings.

PER SERVING: 324 CALORIES (16% FROM FAT)
FAT 5.7G (SATURATED FAT 1.3G)
PROTEIN 30.3G CARBOHYDRATE 36.1G
CHOLESTEROL 70MG SODIUM 186MG

Grill Safety

Don't grill chicken too close to the coals, and try to keep it from being charred by flames. If it is charred, trim off any black pieces before serving.

SESAME CHICKEN KABOBS

5 (4-ounce) skinned, boned chicken breast
　　halves
½ cup low-sodium soy sauce
½ cup commercial nonfat Catalina dressing
¼ cup minced onion
2½ tablespoons lemon juice
1 tablespoon sesame seeds
1 clove garlic, crushed
½ teaspoon ground ginger
1 medium-size green pepper, cut into 1-inch
　　pieces
1 medium-size sweet red pepper, cut into
　　1-inch pieces
1 (8-ounce) can pineapple chunks in juice,
　　drained
Vegetable cooking spray
6 cups cooked long-grain rice (cooked without
　　salt or fat)

Cut chicken into 1-inch cubes; place in a heavy-duty, zip-top plastic bag. Combine soy sauce and next 6 ingredients in a small bowl; stir well. Pour over chicken; seal bag, and shake until chicken is well coated. Marinate in refrigerator 2 hours, turning bag occasionally.

Remove chicken from marinade, reserving marinade. Thread chicken, pepper pieces, and pineapple alternately on 6 (12-inch) skewers. Coat grill rack with cooking spray; place over medium-hot coals. Place kabobs on rack; grill 15 minutes or until chicken is done, turning and basting frequently with marinade. Serve kabobs over rice. Yield: 6 servings.

PER SERVING: 394 CALORIES (9% FROM FAT)
FAT 3.9G (SATURATED FAT 0.9G)
PROTEIN 26.8G CARBOHYDRATE 58.8G
CHOLESTEROL 60MG SODIUM 479MG

Tropical Chicken Kabobs

TROPICAL CHICKEN KABOBS

⅓ cup lime juice
1 tablespoon vegetable oil
1 tablespoon honey
1½ pounds skinned, boned chicken breast, cut
    into 1½-inch pieces
12 pearl onions, peeled
1 large green pepper, seeded and cut into
    2-inch pieces
1 papaya, peeled, seeded, and cut into 2-inch
    pieces
1½ cups fresh pineapple chunks
Vegetable cooking spray

Combine lime juice, vegetable oil, and honey in a shallow dish. Add chicken; toss gently. Cover and marinate in refrigerator 8 hours, stirring occasionally. Remove chicken from marinade, reserving marinade. Alternate chicken, onions, pepper, papaya, and pineapple on 6 (12-inch) skewers. Coat grill rack with cooking spray; place on grill over medium-hot coals. Place kabobs on rack, and grill 15 to 20 minutes or until done, turning and basting frequently with reserved marinade. Yield: 6 servings.

PER SERVING: 222 CALORIES (23% FROM FAT)
FAT 5.7G (SATURATED FAT 1.2G)
PROTEIN 26.6G   CARBOHYDRATE 16.4G
CHOLESTEROL 70MG   SODIUM 66MG

INDEX